WINDOWS 98
QUICK REFERENCE

Keith Powell

201 West 103rd Street, Indianapolis, Indiana 46290

MICROSOFT WINDOWS 98 QUICK REFERENCE
Copyright© 1999 by Que

All rights reserved. No part of this book shall be reproduced, stored in a retrieval system, or transmitted by any means, electronic, mechanical, photocopying, recording, or otherwise, without written permission from the publisher. No patent liability is assumed with respect to the use of the information contained herein. Although every precaution has been taken in the preparation of this book, the publisher and author assume no responsibility for errors nor omissions. Neither is any liability assumed for damages resulting from the use of the information contained herein.

ISBN: 0-7897-2030-2

International ISBN: 0-7897-2088-4

Library of Congress Catalog Card Number: 99-62269

Printed in the United States of America

First Printing: June 1999

01 00 99   4 3 2 1

TRADEMARKS

All terms mentioned in this book that are known to be trademarks or service marks have been appropriately capitalized. Que cannot attest to the accuracy of this information. Use of a term in this book should not be regarded as affecting the validity of any trademark or service mark. Windows is a registered trademark of Microsoft Corporation.

WARNING AND DISCLAIMER

Every effort has been made to make this book as complete and as accurate as possible, but no warranty or fitness is implied. The information provided is on an "as is" basis. The author and the publisher shall have neither liability nor responsibility to any person or entity with respect to any loss or damages arising from the information contained in this book.

Executive Editor Angela Wethington	**Managing Editor** Thomas F. Hayes	**Proofreader** Tricia Sterling
Acquisitions Editor Stephanie McComb	**Project Editor** Lori A. Lyons	**Interior Designer** Louisa Klucznik
Development Editor Valerie Perry	**Copy Editor** Christy Parrish	**Cover Designer** Dan Armstrong
Technical Editor Kyle Bryant	**Indexer** Larry Sweazy	**Layout Technician** Brad Lenser

ACCESSIBILITY OPTIONS

Windows 98 contains a number of accessibility options that are actually enhancements to those found in Windows 95. These features enable individuals with mobility, hearing, and/or visual impairments to use a personal computer without the hassle of installing special equipment. Available options include the following:

- **StickyKeys**—When this feature is enabled, Windows allows the use of the (⇧Shift), (Ctrl), or (Alt) keys in combination with other keys but only requiring one key to be pressed at a time. For example, to perform a copy operation inside Windows 98, you need to be able to press and hold down the Ctrl key while clicking once on the "C" key to copy the highlighted text or object to the Clipboard. With the use of the StickyKeys feature, you are able to perform this keystroke combination with just a single hand.

- **FilterKeys**—When this feature is enabled, Windows will ignore brief or repeated keystrokes, as well as slowing the repeat rate if need be. For example, if you accidentally press and hold down the spacebar, Windows 98 would not necessarily think you wanted more than a single space included in your text.

- **ToggleKeys**—When this feature is enabled, Windows will generate tones when the (Caps Lock), (Num Lock), or (Scroll Lock) keys are pressed. For example, this would make it easier for someone who was visually impaired to know when he is pressing one of these specialty keyboard keys instead of a letter key.

- **SoundSentry**—When this feature is enabled, Windows generates visual indications, such as making your screen blink, when your system makes a sound.

- **ShowSounds**—When this feature is enabled, your programs display captions for words that they speak and sounds that they make. For example, hearing-impaired individuals would no longer be deprived of information that is deployed via the computer speaker instead of being shown on the computer screen. This might be in the form of a beep when you press the wrong key, such that the word "beep" would then be shown on your computer screen.

- **High Contrast**—When this feature is enabled, Windows will use colors and fonts designed for easy reading. For example, you might see black text on a white background or white text on a blue background (these settings are user-controlled).
- **MouseKeys**—When this feature is enabled, you will be able to use your keyboard to control your mouse pointer. This is useful to those persons who may not have the same physical dexterity of others who find it possible to use a mouse pointing device.

Determine the Availability of Accessibility Options

1. Click **Start**, choose **Settings**, and select **Control Panel**, which will then open the Control Panel window.
2. The blue-and-white **Accessibility Options** icon should appear in the Control Panel window. If this icon is not present in the Control Panel window, then it has not yet been installed onto your PC.

NOTE

If the **Accessibility Options** icon was not present in your Control Panel, then you will need to install the applicable programs for it. To do that, refer to the "Add/Remove Programs" section later in this book.

---

3. Confirm the presence of the **Accessibility Options** icon and continue.

See Also Add/Remove Programs

Open Accessibility Options

1. Move the mouse pointer to the **Accessibility Options** icon and single- or double-click the primary mouse button. This opens the Accessibility Properties dialog.

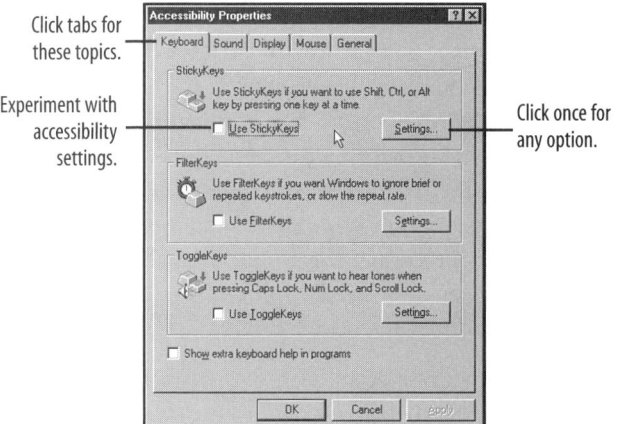

Click tabs for these topics.
Experiment with accessibility settings.
Click once for any option.

2. Clicking once on any of the tabs will then display the possibilities available to you to customize the use of your PC's keyboard, sound device, display monitor, and mouse. The General tab includes the ability to turn off accessibility options that have been left idle for *x* number of minutes.

ACTIVE DESKTOP ENVIRONMENT

In late 1997, Microsoft first introduced the Active Desktop environment that was integrated into the Windows 98 operating system as an add-on component to its Internet Explorer 4.0 Web browser. Having the Active Desktop feature quite simply means that the Windows 98 Desktop can display Web content saved in HTML (Hypertext Markup Language) format and can update it each time you connect to the Internet. For example, suppose you place on your Active Desktop a news site that is updated daily. Each time you connect to the Internet, that news site will be automatically updated on your PC's desktop. Additionally, favorite *channels* can be placed on the Windows 98 Active Desktop.

Viewing your Active Desktop as a Web page permits the use of "active" content directly on the Windows 98 Desktop area. This content can come in the form of HTML (or Web) pages, animated GIF graphics (such as the popular

dancing 7-Up guys found on many Web pages), and so forth. These items will appear to "float" on your desktop, meaning that the normal Windows 98 background graphic appears to be on the bottom level, with the active content appearing next, followed by the normal icons that sit on the desktop (such as the Recycle Bin or My Computer) coming last (or on top). To try this, add a background, place some active content on top of it (such as the Channel Bar), and then drag your Recycle Bin on top of that. See how they all stack? Interesting, isn't it?

If you take this one step further, you can begin to see the Microsoft vision for the desktop. It becomes an extension of the Internet Explorer Web browser or vice versa, meaning that your Internet Explorer Web browser is now your desktop folder and File Manager (for those of you who still remember Windows 3.x, the **File Manager** tool was what you used to manipulate files and directories on your PC). Everything is done in the same way, making Windows 98 that much easier to use while increasing your productivity.

See Also Channels

Implement the Active Desktop Feature

1. Right-click a blank spot on the Windows 98 Desktop to open a shortcut menu, and then click the **Active Desktop** entry to view your **Active Desktop** options.

2. A check mark next to the View as Web Page option indicates that the Active Desktop feature has been enabled, which means that Web content can be saved and activated (used) directly from the Windows 98 Desktop. If no check mark is present, click the View as Web Page option to begin using it.

Customize the Active Desktop

1. Right-click on a blank spot on the Windows 98 Desktop to open the shortcut menu, then click once on the **Active Desktop** menu option, and then click once on the **Customize My Desktop** entry to view your **Active Desktop** options.

2. Select the **Web** tab of the Display Properties dialog.

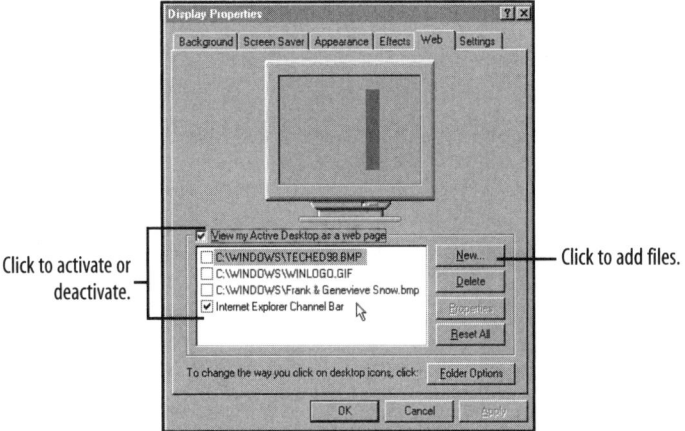

Click to activate or deactivate.
Click to add files.

Add Active Content to Your Desktop

1. Click once on `New`, which will start a small wizard that will walk you through the steps to locate "active" types of files on your computer or on the Internet.

> **NOTE**
> A wizard is an interactive help session that assists you during a configuration process.

2. If your PC is connected to the Internet via a local area network (LAN) connection or a dial-up networking (DUN) connection, you can choose to download additional Windows 98 graphics and Web items directly from the **Active Desktop Gallery** at Microsoft's Web site.

3. If your PC is not connected to the Internet (or if you do not want to visit the Active Desktop Gallery), you should click once on the `No` button when this option is offered to you by the Active Desktop Wizard.

4. During this process, you will also see an **In The Future, Do Not Show Me This Dialog** check box. Click it to avoid seeing that dialog ever again.

5. If you know the exact location of the Active Desktop item you want, type it in the **Location** text. If you do not know the exact location, click [Browse Files...] to scan the hard drive for the desired item.

6. Find the file you seek by selecting its parent drive and folder from the **Look in** drop-down list box of the Browse dialog.

7. When you find the file, click it to select it, and then click [Open] to return to the previous window.

8. The pathname of the file will automatically appear in the **Location** text. Click once on [OK] to continue.

9. The file that you selected is now highlighted and displayed in the **Web** tab of the Display Properties dialog. To accept this change to the Active Desktop, click either [Apply] or [OK].

10. Click [Apply] to stay in the Display Properties dialog and customize the Active Desktop in other ways.

11. Click the [OK] button to apply the change and return to the Windows 98 Desktop.

See Also Dial-Up Networking

ADD NEW HARDWARE WIZARD

When you add new hardware to a computer, a piece of software is required as well. This software is known as either a *driver* or a software driver. A software driver functions similarly to a person driving a car. That is, when you act as the driver for your car, you control certain aspects of the automobile's operation. For example, turning the steering wheel causes the car to move in a particular direction, while pressing the gas or brake pedals results in the auto moving faster or slower, and turning the ignition key causes the car's engine to start (well, usually anyway, except maybe my car). Think of a software driver in the same fashion: it will control how a particular piece of hardware will react to the commands being processed by the computer's brain (a.k.a.,

its CPU). For example, your computer cannot just tell the printer to print without first interfacing at the machine or hardware level with the printer. This is where the software driver(s) for that printer comes into play (yes, it is possible for a single hardware device to have multiple drivers, but you do not have to worry about that...Windows 98 automatically handles all of those types of issues). The software drivers will process the commands for printing your document from your computer, which will then result in your document appearing on the printer.

To include the software drivers necessary for adding hardware such as a new modem, DVD-ROM drive, or network interface card, you may need to use the Windows 98 Add New Hardware Wizard. If you are installing PnP (Plug and Play) hardware, then Windows 98 may automatically recognize this hardware. This would then mean that you would not need to run the Add New Hardware Wizard.

ADD NEW HARDWARE

1. Click **Start**, choose **Settings**, **Control Panel**, which will cause the Windows 98 Control Panel window to appear.
2. Double-click the **Add New Hardware** icon in the Control Panel to start the **Add New Hardware** Wizard.
3. Before continuing with the wizard, be sure to close any running applications.
4. Click **Next>** in the wizard's initial window.

> **NOTE**
>
> It is possible that this wizard will start automatically when you start up your system, especially if the hardware you have added is installed inside the CPU box of your Windows 98 computer (such as a new hard drive, CD-ROM device, or internal modem).

5. Windows 98 will search first for Plug and Play devices and then for non–Plug and Play devices.

> **NOTE**
> A Plug and Play device is simply a hardware component that is automatically recognized by the Windows 98 operating system. Of course, a Plug and Play device is a bit more than just that. It is a hardware component that has been specifically designed to work with Windows 98 in such a way that its system resources are freed automatically when you disable or remove that device from your system.

6. Click `Next >` to instruct Windows 98 to conduct the search.

> **NOTE**
> If you are not trying to install a Plug and Play device, the Windows 98 search will fail. It is at this point that Windows 98 asks you whether you want it to search for non–Plug and Play hardware.

7. The **Yes** radio button is selected by default, which instructs Windows 98 to search for non–Plug and Play devices. If you know exactly what software drivers you want to install, it is much faster to click the **No, I Want to Select the Hardware from a List** radio button and then click `Next >` to continue.

8. Use the scrollbar along the right side of the window to view all the **Hardware Types** menu choices. If the device you want to install does not appear to be listed, click the **Other Devices** option then click `Next >` to select your device's manufacturer and model.

9. Use the scrollbars to view the devices available for installation. Locate the device that you are attempting to install, click on it once to select it, and then click `Next >` to continue.

> **NOTE**
> This is a good way to determine whether that new, snazzy piece of telephonic equipment that you have your eye on is compatible with Windows 98 (if it is, chances are it will show up somewhere in these lists).

NOTE

If you have the floppy disk(s) or CD-ROM containing the Windows 98 software drivers required for your new device, click the `Have Disk...` button to continue the process.

10. Click `Finish` to complete the process. You might be prompted to restart your PC. If you are prompted, then you should definitely do so because Windows 98 often will not install a device correctly if you refuse to restart your machine, and instead, will continue working on other things on your PC.

11. To determine whether the hardware device has installed properly (following the restart process, if it was required), double-click the **System** icon in the Control Panel.

12. After the System Properties dialog appears, click once on the **Device Manager** tab.

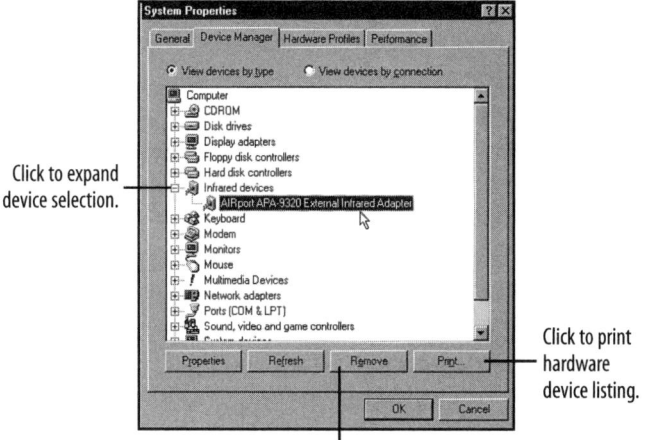

Click to expand device selection.

Click to print hardware device listing.

Click to remove device.

ADD A PRINTER WIZARD

Adding a new printer to a computer used to be rather complex, especially when you had to get all the applications installed on that PC to work correctly with the new printer. Under Windows 95, that changed because of the **Add Printer** Wizard. In Windows 98, this same wizard still exists, although in all fairness to Microsoft it does appear to run more smoothly than it did in Windows 95.

Run the Add a Printer Wizard

1. Click [Start], choose **Settings**, **Printers**.
2. Double-click the **Add Printer** icon to start the wizard.
3. In the first window of the Add Printer Wizard, just click [Next>] to continue.
4. In this next window, specify how the printer is attached to your PC. Make your selection, and then click [Next>] to continue.

> **NOTE**
>
> A local printer is physically attached to your computer via a parallel printer cable (also known as a centronix cable) or possibly a serial cable. In the case of a network connection, both the network printer and your PC are physically attached to a network device, such as a hub or a concentrator, or one that is connected via another PC to the local network. If the computer is a home computer or a laptop (and you are not at the office), then there is approximately a 99.999% chance that it uses a local printer, not a network printer.

5. To determine the make and model of the printer you are installing, look on the cover of the instruction manual that came with the printer or on the print device itself.
6. Select your printer's manufacturer from the **Manufacturers** list, and then select your printer's model from the **Printers** list. Click [Next>] to continue.
7. Make sure the printer is plugged in and turned on.

8. Connect the parallel print cable into the parallel port (also know as LPT1) on the back of your PC.

> **NOTE**
> If you happen to own a 10- or 20-year-old serial printer, you would plug its cable into one of the serial ports on the back of your PC (typically, this would be a nine-pin connector, but it is possible to have a larger serial port connector).

9. Unless your printer is a serial port device, make sure the LPT1 option is selected in the Available ports list. Click [Next >] to continue.

> **NOTE**
> If you are attempting to connect a serial port device, such as an older dot-matrix printer that is connected to one of the COMx: ports (a.k.a., a serial port) on your PC, then the correct choice here will be the exact serial communications port where the printer cable is connected. For example, if you have connected the serial printer cable to your computer's COMx: port (where x equals the serial port number such as 1 or 2), then the correct option to select in the **Available ports** list should correspond to this port number. If the back of your PC uses letters instead of numbers to describe the COM ports, then COMa: is really the same thing as COM1:, and so on.

10. Type a descriptive name for the printer in the **Printer Name** text box. If you want Windows 98 to use this printer by default, click the **Yes** radio button. (If you already have at least one printer installed on your PC, this window will default to the **No** radio button automatically.) Click [Next >] to continue.

11. If you want to print a test page to ensure that the printer has been installed correctly, make sure the **Yes** radio button is selected and click [Finish].

> **NOTE**
>
> After you click [Finish], Windows 98 will probably want to install some new software printer drivers before placing the new print device inside the **Printers** window. Keep in mind that Windows 98 might prompt you to insert your Windows 98 CD-ROM disc in the computer's CD-ROM disc drive should it require additional files that do not already exist on your computer's hard disk drive. If you are presented with a dialog such as this, simply insert the CD-ROM disc and then click [OK] to affirm that the CD is now properly placed in the correct location. (Note that on some PCs, once you place the CD in the drive, Windows 98 will automatically detect it and perform its magic for you.)

12. If you can read the printout, then the printer has been installed correctly. If not, it is possible that you installed the wrong driver; if this is the case, you should carefully repeat these steps.

13. Return to the Printers window by clicking [Start], then choose **Settings**, **Printers**. The newly installed print device should be present. The **check mark** icon next to the newly installed printer indicates that that printer is the default print device for that PC.

> **NOTE**
>
> The **Printers** window will display all the print devices that have been installed on your computer, including actual printers, fax devices, and other telephonic print devices. The check mark inside the black circle means that this is the "default" printer for this computer. The small outstretched hand that appears to be holding the printer means that this printer is "Shared" to other network users.

See Also Printers

ADD/REMOVE PROGRAMS

A Windows 98 *component/utility/accessory* is a piece of software that comes with the Windows 98 operating system at the time of purchase. A Windows 98 *program* or *application* is a non-Windows 98 piece of software that does not come in the same box as Windows 98 did. For example, Microsoft Money 98 is a home finance software application that can be both installed and deleted from your PC using the Add/Remove Programs dialog, but it is a distinctly separate piece of software from anything found inside Windows 98. Likewise, applications are installed/deleted by using the **Install/Uninstall** tab, while all Windows 98 components, utilities, and/or accessories will be installed or removed by using the **Windows Setup** tab.

The Windows 98 Add/Remove Programs feature enables you to easily add and remove programs as well as Windows 98 components.

When it comes to adding new programs or components, you have two options:

- Install an application, such as Microsoft Office, by clicking [Install...].
- Install Windows 98 components that are not installed in your version of Windows 98.

> **NOTE**
>
> To remove a built-in Windows 98 accessory, utility, or component, simply use the same process that you use to install the application, only in reverse. For example, to remove the **Web TV for Windows** component that is added in the following example, simply uncheck the **Web TV for Windows** check box in the **Windows Setup** tab of the **Add/Remove Programs Properties** dialog and then click OK . Windows 98 will automatically uninstall this component and delete any unnecessary files.

Access Add/Remove Programs

1. Click Start, choose **Settings, Control Panel**.
2. Double-click the **Add/Remove Programs** icon in the **Control Panel** to start yet another Windows 98 wizard.
3. There are a couple options in the **Install/Uninstall** tab of the **Add/Remove Programs Properties** dialog.

   - You can install new applications or Windows 98 components.
   - You can remove installed software from your hard drive.

   This window contains a listing of all the Windows 98-compliant applications that are already installed on your PC. To add or remove Windows 98 operating system components, click on the **Windows Setup** tab to move to that screen of the Add/Remove Programs utility.

Add New Programs or Windows 98 Components

1. Click the **Windows Setup** tab to display the full list of Windows 98 add-on components (components need not be installed on your computer to be displayed in this list).
2. Scroll to the **Web TV for Windows** option and click its check box.

Click to add or remove features.

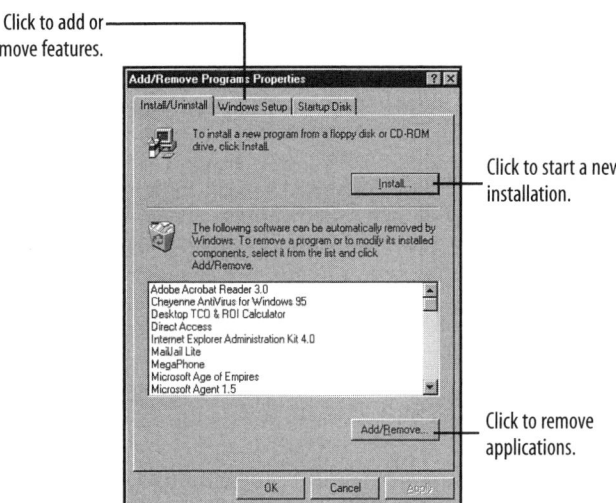

Click to start a new installation.

Click to remove applications.

> **NOTE**
>
> Next to each component, a check box appears. If a box containing a check mark is shaded, it means that only some of that component's options have been installed. If the checked box has a white background, it means that all of that component's options have been installed. To change a box from gray to white, simply click a gray box to deselect it and then click it again. It should appear white, indicating that all the component's options are installed. If you do not check all the options available to you, then you are selectively installing or uninstalling a component.

3. Click **OK** to continue the installation process.
4. Windows 98 will prompt you to insert the Windows 98 CD-ROM if the appropriate files do not exist on your hard drive.
5. Insert the CD-ROM and click **OK** to continue. Windows 98 will display a Progress dialog that will indicate those files that are being installed onto your computer's hard drive, as well as also showing you just how far along the installation process is.

> **NOTE**
>
> If a Version Conflict dialog appears, it is usually best to keep the file in question. Unfortunately, there is no perfect method for knowing which version is the best one to keep. When in doubt, always keep your original file. You can always go back and reinstall the software application (that you are presently trying to install) should this be an improper choice. Windows 98 will try to advise you the best course of action, by telling you its recommendation within the text of this dialog (look closely at the last line of the top paragraph).

6. You might be asked to restart your computer to complete the process. If you want your new settings to take effect immediately, close all active programs and then click the **Yes** radio button to restart your PC. If you do not restart your PC when prompted, that particular application might not function properly.

Remove Applications and Windows 98 Components

1. Click the **Install/Uninstall** tab of the **Add/Remove Programs Properties** dialog. To uninstall any of these programs, select the one you want to delete (in this example, **Windows 98 Uninstall Information** is selected), and then click OK.

> **NOTE**
>
> The **Windows 98 Uninstall Information** option permits you to uninstall Windows 98 if it is an upgrade to a previously existing version of Windows (3.1 or 95). If you decide that you do not want to remove Windows 98 now or in the future, it is wise to uninstall this program to save space. Removing the **Windows 98 Uninstall Information** option will also prevent you from accidentally deleting the Windows 98 operating system and going back to an older version of Windows. If you do decide to try to return to a previous operating system, you may need to reinstall many of your new applications. Also, if you have upgraded to FAT32, you will not be able to return to a previous version of Windows.

2. Click Yes in the dialog to confirm that you want to remove this program.

3. Windows 98 will confirm that the appropriate files have been deleted.

4. Windows 98 then returns you to the **Add/Remove Programs Properties** dialog, where the **Delete Windows 98 Uninstall Information** option is no longer present.

AMERICA ONLINE (AOL)

America Online is one of five online services (AT&T WorldNet, CompuServe, Prodigy Internet, and The Microsoft Network are the others) that can be installed as part of the Windows 98 operating system. When Windows 98 is installed, pointers to these five services are installed to ensure the availability of the software for these services. To install any or all of these services, except The Microsoft Network whose icon is surprisingly placed directly on the Windows 98 Desktop (what a coincidence, eh?), you must open the Online Service folder.

Install America Online

1. After you're inside the Online Services folder, double-click the **America Online** service to begin the installation process.

2. You are presented with four installation buttons:
   - **America Online**
   - **AOL UK**
   - **AOL Canada**
   - **Information**

3. Click once on a ⬤ button to initiate the country-specific installation of America Online. If you live someplace other than one of these three nations, click once on the Information button to receive instructions on what to do next.

4. Follow the remaining America Online installation prompts. Upon completion, you will be required to restart your PC. Do so to complete the installation process.

5. After your computer finishes restarting, you will see a new shortcut on your Windows 98 desktop labeled "AOL & Internet FREE Trial!". Double-click on that icon to start using America Online.

See Also AT&T WorldNet, CompuServe, Microsoft Network, Prodigy Internet

AT&T WORLDNET SERVICE

AT&T WorldNet is one of five online services (America Online, CompuServe, Prodigy Internet, and The Microsoft Network are the others) that can be installed as part of the Windows 98 operating system. When Windows 98 is installed, pointers to these five services are installed to ensure the availability of the software for these services. To install any or all of these services, except the Microsoft Network whose icon is located directly on the Windows 98 Desktop, you must open the Online Service folder.

Install AT&T WorldNet

1. After you're inside the Online Services folder, double-click the **AT&T WorldNet** icon to start its installation process. A small informational box will appear asking you to wait (actually, you do not have a choice but to wait, so try to be patient while the AT&T software starts to load).

2. After a few seconds, your whole computer screen will be consumed by the AT&T WorldNet service's splash and startup window. There is no clear way to cancel out of this window (other than doing Ctrl+Alt+Del, selecting the AT&T WorldNet service, and then clicking on End Task). There is a misleading hyperlink that will do this, but it is not easy to decipher for a beginning user of Windows 98.

3. To sign up for the AT&T WorldNet service and start its installation process, click once on the **"Click Here to Sign up for AT&T WorldNet Service"** hyperlink.

4. Follow the rest of the AT&T WorldNet Service's installation instructions to complete the installation process. Upon completion, you may be required to restart your PC. Do so to finish the installation process.

See Also America Online, CompuServe, Microsoft Network, Prodigy Internet

BACKUP

The **Backup** option that comes with the Windows 98 operating system is very powerful. It permits you to save your computer data files, applications, graphics, and so on to a variety of media devices such as tape, removable disks, hard drives, and the like. The biggest improvement of this software over the Windows 95 version is that it allows users to back up to a SCSI-connected (Small Computer Systems Interface) device such as a tape drive. The purpose of the Windows 98 backup software is to help protect you from data loss in case your PC breaks down.

Before starting Backup, make sure that the backup hardware device has already been correctly installed and is operational. If you are backing up your data to either a floppy disk or the hard drive, then it is okay to start the backup software at any time.

See Also Add New Hardware Wizard

Start Backup

1. To start the Windows 98 Backup process, click the ![Start] button, choose **Programs**, **Accessories**, **System Tools**, and then select **Backup**.

2. You will subsequently be prompted with three choices:
   - To create a new backup job
   - To open a backup set that you created previously
   - To restore files from a previous backup session

   Because this is the first time that we are running the Backup program, the default choice to create a new backup job is the correct selection. To continue, click once on the ![OK] button.

3. You are then prompted for the *size* of the backup job. You must specify whether you want to back up your entire computer or specific preselected files. Make the default setting, **Back up My Computer**, your selection, and then click once on the ![Next >] button to continue.

4. Back up all the files on your computer or back up any files that have been created or changed since the previous backup. Because we have not yet performed a backup, the default, **All selected files**, is the most appropriate choice. Click once on the [Next >] button to continue.

5. Specify to where these files should be backed up. The default is to save all files to the root directory of C:\; however, this is a bad idea because things get messy when you use the root directory for nonessential files. Instead, you might want to save your backup job, called MyBackup.qic by default, in a specially created folder called C:\MyData. Click once on the [Next >] button to continue.

6. Specify how to back up. You have the following options:

    - Compare original and backup files to verify data was successfully backed up. It is wise to select this option because it verifies that the job was successful.

    - Compress the backup data to save space. This option is useful because it alters the manner in which data is stored so that files require less space than normal.

> **TIP**
>
> Both of these options will slow the backup process; if you are in a hurry, you might want to skip either or both of them.

7. After you have set these parameters, click once on the [Next >] button to continue. The ensuing window enables you to give your backup job a name (Untitled is the default). When you are satisfied with the name, click the [Start] button to continue.

> **TIP**
>
> I suggest using a date-naming scheme so that you can quickly and easily sort through backups. Simply put today's date in a *YYMMDD* format, (where *YY* = the last two digits of the current year, *MM* = the two digits for the current month, and *DD* = the two digits for the current day). For example, as I write this chapter, the date is February 28, 1999, which translates to 990228.

8. The Backup Progress dialog appears automatically as soon as the file and size estimates are complete.

9. Wait until the backup process completes before clicking on the `Report` button. You will know the process is done when the Microsoft Backup dialog appears.

10. Click the `OK` button once to return to the **Backup Progress** dialog that you were just looking at.

11. Click the `Report` button to view and print a summary of the Backup Progress dialog, should you want to keep a hard copy of each of your backup jobs.

12. Click the `OK` button once to end this backup process and return to the Microsoft Backup window.

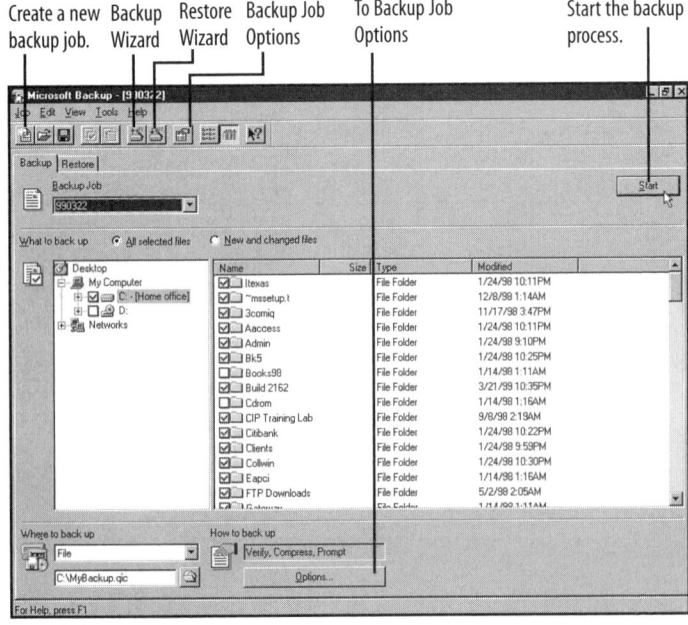

Create a new backup job.   Backup Wizard   Restore Wizard   Backup Job Options   To Backup Job Options   Start the backup process.

NOTE

Checked boxes indicate that those drives and folders are set to be backed up the next time the backup job is executed. You can select any combination of hard drives, folders, and files.

13. Click the [Options...] button to view the Backup Job Options dialog.

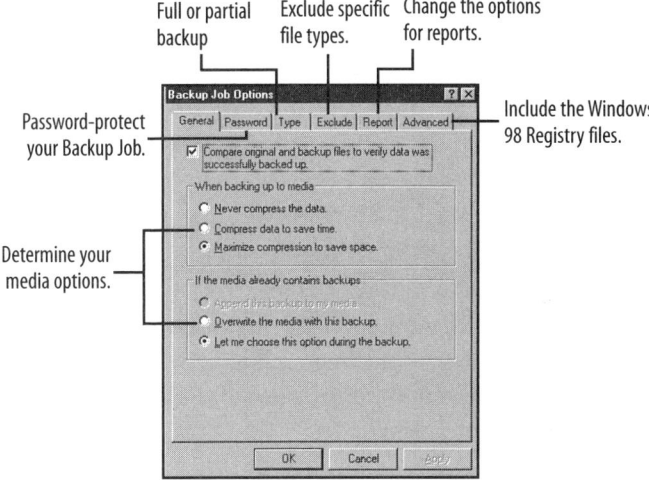

14. Click the [OK] button once to return to the Backup dialog.
15. To exit, click once on the × located in the upper-right corner of the window or click once on the **Job** menu option and then click again on the **Exit** menu selection.

BRIEFCASE

The Briefcase component of Windows 98 aids you in the arduous task of keeping multiple versions of your files in synch between your desktop PC and your laptop or other Windows 98 mobile computer device, such as a notebook, Windows CE device (be it a hand held or palm device), Palm Pilot (or one of the dozen other proprietary versions of hand-held computing hardware that does essentially the same thing), flattop, portable, luggable, and so on.

Obviously, if you only possess a single Windows 98 PC, then this feature is probably irrelevant to you. However, if you are like countless other road warriors out there, the **Briefcase** option will be very useful to you.

Use the Briefcase

1. Double-click the **Briefcase** icon found on the Windows 98 desktop to open it.
2. Drag your important files (that exist elsewhere on your Windows 98 PC) from the Windows Explorer and then drop them onto the Briefcase.
3. Make a copy of the Briefcase by dragging a copy of it to the floppy drive (or Zip, Jaz, SyQuest, PCMCIA hard drive, or other type of device). You may also make a copy of the Briefcase by copying it to your portable Windows 98 computer using your organization's network.
4. As you alter these important files, make sure that you are using the versions that are found inside the Briefcase and not other versions that might reside elsewhere on your computer.
5. When you return from your trip, drag that Briefcase back onto your Windows 98 desktop, and click once on the **Update All** option. This will resynchronize all of your portable computer's Briefcase files with your desktop computer's Briefcase files.

Microsoft provides a calculator within Windows 98. The Calculator program offers two types of calculators:

- **Standard**—This is probably the type of calculator you're used to and have used for years; it is most useful for calculations using the decimal number system.
- **Scientific**—This type of calculator supports a variety of numbering systems such as hexadecimal, decimal, octal, and binary.

Access Calculator

1. Click once on the [Start] button, then choose **Programs**, **Accessories**, and **Calculator**.

> **NOTE**
>
> The standard calculator feature will probably appear first (unless you have already used the calculator in its scientific mode, in which case it will display that mode by default). This calculator works just like the one you have at home. You can press the numeric keys on your computer's keyboard, if you do not want to use the mouse. The standard calculator contains all the basic arithmetic and memory functions, along with a few extras—such as the capability to calculate square roots, percents, and the reciprocal of a number.

2. To switch to the scientific calculator, click the **View** menu option and then click **Scientific**.
3. The scientific calculator offers a host of features and functions that are probably better explained in a math book. To switch back to the standard calculator, simply click once on the **View** menu option and then choose the **Standard** menu feature.
4. To close the Windows 98 Calculator, click once on the × button in the upper-right corner of the program's window.

CD PLAYER

To use the CD Player feature of Windows 98, you must have three things:

- A CD-ROM drive in your PC
- A usable sound card and speakers (the speakers do not have to be external devices, as in the case of most laptops)
- A music compact disc

Operate CD Player

1. Put your music CD into your CD-ROM drive.
2. Start the CD Player software by clicking the [Start] button and choosing **Programs**, **Accessories**, **Entertainment**, and then **CD Player**. It is possible for the music CD to begin playing automatically, if the auto-insert feature of Windows 98 is activated on your PC.
3. The Windows 98 CD Player window opens.

4. Display the toolbar by clicking the **View** menu and selecting **Toolbar**. The toolbar will then appear along the top of the CD Player window.
5. To change the volume, click on the **View** menu option and select **Volume Control**. The Volume Control window will then open (review the "Volume Control" option later in this book for more details on its proper usage).

6. To close CD Player, click the × button in the upper-right corner of the window.

See Also Add New Hardware

CHANNELS

In Windows 98 terminology, a *channel* is a Web site designed to push its content to your PC according to the schedule you set. Channels enable you to receive regular updates to certain Web sites without having to navigate around the Internet to find them.

The Channel bar should already be present on the Active Desktop. If it is not, refer to the "Active Desktop" section to learn how to display it.

Hover your mouse pointer over a button in the Channel bar, such as the [channel guide] button. Windows 98 will automatically display information about the feature that you are hovering over (this display of information is commonly referred to as a *ToolTip*).

Operate Channel Bar

1. Make sure that you are connected to the Internet, and then click the [channel guide] button at the top of the Channel bar.
2. This opens the default browser (usually Microsoft's Internet Explorer, although America Online's Netscape Navigator typically works as well) and displays the Microsoft Active Channel Guide as the default site. However, keep in mind that older versions of America Online's Navigator and Communicator Web browsers might not work as well as Microsoft's Internet Explorer Web browser.
3. Click any channel category that appears along the left side of the window, such as the **Lifestyle and Travel** category.

> **TIP**
>
> Hover over any channel and you will be presented with information about that particular channel in the form of a tool tip.

4. Right-click a channel from within a channel category to open the **Subscription** menu. Click once on the **Subscribe** command to start the channel subscription process.

> **NOTE**
>
> A channel subscription means that you may receive regular updates of a particular channel's contents on some prescribed basis that you determine. When you do this, various files will start to copy themselves onto your PC.

5. In the Modify Channel Usage dialog, you will be asked if you want to subscribe to this Internet channel and, if so, at what level. To subscribe to the channel and to customize how often downloads occur, select the Schedule radio button. Then click the [Customize] button.
6. The first screen of the Windows 98 Subscription Wizard opens. Specify whether you want to download only the home page for the channel or all of its content and then click once on the [Next >] button.
7. If you want to be notified via email when the page has changed, click the **Yes** radio button. If you do not want to be notified, choose the **No** option. Click once on the [Next >] button when you've made your selection.

> **TIP**
>
> To change the default email address, click on the **Change Address** button. You are then prompted to enter another email address along with the outbound or outgoing SMTP (simple mail transfer protocol) email server name that you need to obtain from either your ISP or your company's system administrator. Click on the [OK] button to return to the Subscription Wizard screen.

8. Click once on the **Scheduled** radio button to select an automated schedule from the adjacent drop-down list. Alternatively, you can always click once on the **Manually** radio button to set your own pace.
9. Click the [Finish] button to complete the wizard and return to the Web browser screen.
10. To open a channel, right-click on the channel to view its shortcut menu, and then click once on the **Open Channel** option. The channel you chose appears within your Web browser window. This is also an easy way to preview channels before subscribing to them.
11. When you have finished, close the browser by clicking the × button in the upper-right corner of the browser window.

See Also Active Desktop, Dial-Up Networking

CHARACTER MAP

The Windows 98 Character Map offers a quick and easy way to add special characters (such as a ©, ®, J, and more) to whatever application you might be using, such as a word processor, spreadsheet, or graphical tool.

Apply Symbols and Characters

1. Click once on the [Start] button, then choose **Programs**, **Accessories**, **System Tools**, and then **Character Map**.
2. Click once on a symbol in the Character Map window to make it larger and easier to view. To place a character in the **Characters to copy** text box, either double-click the character or single-click to select it, and then click the [Select] button.

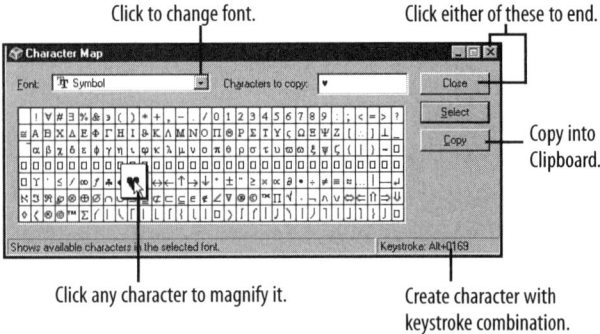

Click to change font.
Click either of these to end.
Copy into Clipboard.
Click any character to magnify it.
Create character with keystroke combination.

CLIPBOARD

The Clipboard within the Windows 98 operating system is used as a holding or staging area for either graphics or text that has been copied onto it. Think of the Clipboard area as a spot within the memory of your computer that holds information that you have copied (perhaps through a cut and paste function), but have not yet pasted or moved to its new location. Please note that although you might have already pasted whatever was on the Clipboard, a copy of it remains there until you either grab something else or shutdown Windows 98.

The Clipboard Viewer accessory (discussed next) is a Windows 98 utility that permits you to "see" exactly what is in the Clipboard holding area at any time. This can make it easier for you to manage your cutting and pasting operations, should you be copying and/or moving large graphical images around your computer system.

CLIPBOARD VIEWER

The Microsoft Clipboard Viewer for Windows 98 enables you to see those items that you have copied to the Clipboard. Items copied to the Clipboard can then be pasted into other Windows applications, such as Microsoft Word, Microsoft PowerPoint, Visio, and so on.

Access the Clipboard Viewer

1. Click once on the **Start** button, choose **Programs, Accessories, System Tools**, and then select **Clipboard Viewer**.
2. The Clipboard Viewer window appears, showing all the special characters and graphics that are presently saved on the Clipboard.

> **TIP**
>
> Whenever Windows 98 is shut down or restarted, all the contents of the Clipboard are discarded. Be sure to paste the Clipboard's contents to a Windows application before shutting down your system.

CLOSING WINDOWS 98

Before you stop using a PC that is running the Windows 98 operating system, you must shut it down or "close" it properly. To do this, click once on the **Start** button and then select the **Shut Down** menu selection (it is the one at the bottom of the list). Should you fail to close the Windows 98 operating system in this manner (for example, you decide to simply power-off your PC), there is a very good possibility for you to lose data that you thought you had already saved to your hard drive through one of your applications, including database-based programs.

CODEC

The Windows 98 term **CODEC** simply means Compression/*Decompression* (see how they derived this acronym?). A CODEC is used for audio and video files in such a manner that it permits your computer to more effectively manage its multimedia functions. As a user of Windows 98, you do not need to worry about CODECs because the operating system will automatically do this for you. However, if you want to impress your friends by talking about CODECs, one of the more popular CODEC formats is the MPEG format.

COMIC (MICROSOFT) CHAT

There is a neat utility that comes packaged with the Windows 98 operating system known as Microsoft Comic Chat. (You will want to download the updated version of this application from Microsoft's Windows 98 Windows Update Internet Web site.) Comic Chat permits a Windows 98 user to talk (through keyboard writing) with others in an Internet chat room. What makes Comic Chat so special is that it is visual. This means that everyone appears as a comic book character (although it is possible to remain in a plain text format, should your computer or Internet connection not be powerful enough to support the comical characters). One can modify their own character to give it a range of emotions, as well as to give it a "life" of its own. Chat sessions can also be saved and/or printed for future reference.

To use the Comic Chat application, you first need to connect to the Internet.

Set Up and Use Microsoft Comic Chat

1. After the connection has been established, click once on the **Start** button, move the mouse pointer to **Programs**, **Internet Tools**, and then click on the **Microsoft Chat** menu selection. The Microsoft Chat application opens.

> **NOTE**
>
> If this is the first time that you have used this Windows 98 utility, the Chat Connection window appears. If this is not your first time using Microsoft Chat, then you will go directly to the Connect window upon starting the Microsoft Chat software. When you first see the Chat Connection screen, the Connect tab will be displayed. Unless you know of other chat servers on the Internet, as well as other chat rooms, it is advised that the first-time user leave the defaults in place. Otherwise, you could click on the drop-down list box to access other Microsoft Chat servers that are available to you.

2. Three radio button options appear at the bottom of the first screen. If this is your first time, it is strongly suggested that you leave the default setting for accessing the **#Comic_Chat** room. You can select from a listing of all the available chat rooms by clicking once on the middle radio button, or you can just connect to the server (but not enter any rooms) by clicking the bottom radio button.
3. After you have made your choice, click once on the **Personal Info** tab to continue.
4. Type in a descriptive name for yourself or your real name, as well as a fun nickname. You should use a real email address in the third box from the top.

> **NOTE**
>
> Your Internet Web page URL and your email address are optional fields. The **Brief Description of Yourself** box at the bottom is a good place to put some quote or saying that you like (if you leave this blank, Windows 98 will force a quote in there that says that "you are too lazy to write one for yourself").

> **NOTE**
>
> The **Nickname** field is the only required entry on the **Personal Info** tab. However, there are a few things to remember. The chat software does not accept illegal characters, such as periods and commas; and will therefore slap you with an error message anytime you try to use those types of characters. It is recommended that you try to limit yourself to only characters and numbers for your nicknames and refrain from attempting to use special characters, spaces, and punctuation marks.

5. Click once on the **Character** tab to continue the configuration process.
6. Preview your "new" self. Click once on any character name in the box on the left to preview a comic character in the box to the right. Click once on the heads in the circle to change the face of your character. Place

the mouse pointer on top of each face (without clicking to generate a description of what the mood is for that particular head).

7. Click on the background of your choice, and you will see a preview of it in the window to the right.

8. After you have made all your selections, click once on the [OK] button to save your choices. The Chat Connection window will close and you will finally enter the Microsoft Chat application.

> **NOTE**
>
> After the Microsoft Chat main window appears, you will be able to start your chat session(s). Unfortunately, if you forgot to connect to the Internet first, this screen will be blank until you establish that all-critical connection to the Internet. After you make that connection, you will be able to use this interesting application fully.
>
> The first time you do actually connect to the Microsoft Chat application server, you might encounter an `Enter New Nickname` error message and repair box. This error means that someone else has already thought of your Microsoft Chat nickname. To fix it, pick another name because you will not be permitted to connect to the Microsoft Chat servers until you have chosen a unique nickname.

9. Click once on the [OK] button to start using the Microsoft Chat application.

10. The **Message of the Day** message box appears on your PC. You may click once on the [OK] button to make this message box disappear until the next time you enter the chat application. Otherwise, you can click once on the check box in the lower left corner of the message box to prevent this screen from reappearing.

11. After you have made your decision (and selection), click once on the [OK] button to close this screen. You are now an active character within the Microsoft Chat application.

Change chat rooms.   This is you.   List of users on server

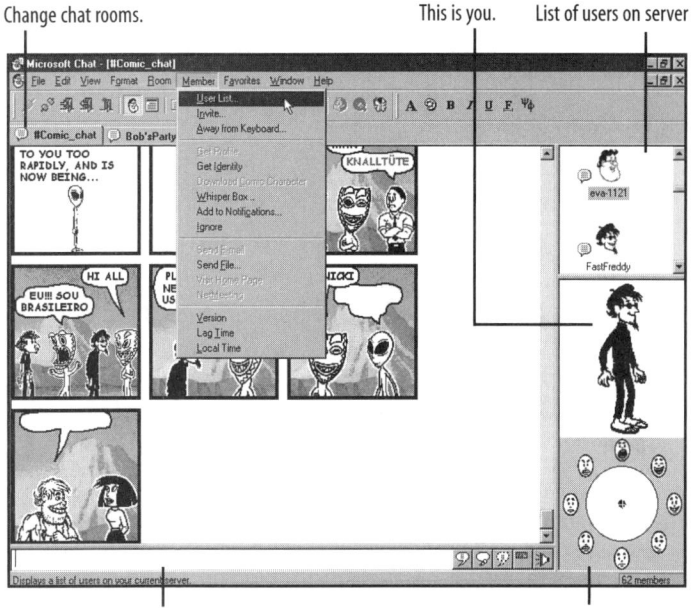

To see yourself say something   Change facial expressions.

12. Finally, to leave the Microsoft Chat session, either click once on the **Room** menu and then select the **Disconnect** feature, or just close the Microsoft Chat application down.

See Also Dial-Up Networking

COMPUTER NAME

The Windows 98 Computer Name acts as the identity for your PC when it is present on a computer network (such as your organization's LAN/WAN). Like most of the other networking configurations that need to be performed in the Windows 98 operating system, this system identification parameter is set from inside the **Network** dialog. This change will take effect only upon restarting your Windows 98 PC. The total time it takes to change this information is about five minutes (and that would be on a bad day), so follow these steps and soon your computer will have a new networking identity.

Identify Your Computer

1. Access the Windows 98 **Control Panel** by first clicking on the [Start] button and then selecting **Settings, Control Panel**.
2. In the Control Panel window, double-click on the **Network** icon to reveal the Network dialog.
3. After the Network dialog appears, click the **Identification** tab. This tab presents you with the opportunity to modify three options: the Computer Name, the Workgroup name, and/or the Computer Description.

> **NOTE**
>
> The name of the computer must be unique, not exceed 15 characters (numbers and letters are acceptable), and should probably not use spaces or any of the other NetBIOS-reserved characters.
>
> The name of the **Workgroup** should be the same as the networking domain that you most often connect to, or it should be the same as the domain of the server that authenticates you to the network. Like the **Computer Name**, it cannot exceed 15 characters (numbers and letters are acceptable).
>
> Do not attempt to set the **Computer Name** and the **Workgroup** name as the same. Windows 98 demands that these two fields contain different names.
>
> The **Computer Description** field should contain a descriptive comment for this user or PC. Although it does not have to be filled-in, you should probably put in some text that most accurately describes the user or computer for consistency.

4. After you have made all your changes and/or entries, click once on the [OK] button to save your changes and exit the **Network** dialog.
5. You will be prompted to restart your Windows 98 computer system. Click once on the [Yes] button to permit the restart process to begin. When your system finishes restarting, you will discover that your newly configured **Computer Name** and/or **Workgroup** name have now taken effect.

COMPRESSION AGENT

Compression Agent enables you to free hard drive disk space without adding an extra hard drive. You free disk space with Compression Agent by compressing your files or by altering the level of the current compression rate.

> **NOTE**
>
> Although you can use the Compression Agent to compress files, there is a catch: You cannot compress drives using the FAT32 storage format. FAT32 is better than FAT16 in that FAT32 stores information on your hard drive more efficiently than does FAT16. The side benefit of this is the appearance of more drive space to the user. However, if your hard drive is less than 512MB in size (a tiny drive when compared to today's standards), then FAT16 must be used, as it will not be possible for you to format such a small drive to the FAT32 format.

See Also FAT32 Drive Converter

Compress a Hard Disk Drive

1. Click the **Start** button, choose **Programs**, **Accessories**, **System Tools**, and then select **Compression Agent** in that order.
2. The Compression Agent window will appear. To start the compression process, click the **Start** button.
3. This tool can take several hours to run so you should not use your computer for any other functions while this utility is operating.

COMPUSERVE

CompuServe, an America Online subsidiary, is one of the Online services (AOL, AT&T WorldNet Service, Prodigy Internet, and The Microsoft Network are the others) that can be installed as part of the Windows 98 operating system. When Windows 98 is installed, pointers to these five services are installed to ensure the availability of the software for these services.

Install CompuServe

1. After you're inside the Online Services folder, double-click the **CompuServe** icon to start its installation process. A small informational box will appear asking you to insert your Windows 98 CD-ROM disc into your CD-ROM disc drive. This is because the CompuServe software requires a file (CS3KIT.EXE) from that CD.

2. Follow the rest of the CompuServe's installation instructions to complete the installation process. Upon completion, you will probably be required to restart your PC. Do so to complete the installation process.

See Also AOL, AT&T WorldNet Service, Microsoft Network, Prodigy Internet

CONTROL PANEL

The Windows 98 Control Panel is the heart of the configuration area for the operating system. In it, you will find all the major system components, and the tools required for their configuration and usage.

Access the Control Panel and Its Components

1. Click the [Start] button, and choose **Settings**, **Control Panel** to open the Control Panel window.

2. The Control Panel window contains icons representing a number of tools, all of which are discussed in the following table.

Tool	Description
Add New Hardware	This Windows 98 wizard helps you properly install the necessary software drivers for new hardware components.
Add/Remove Programs	This Windows 98 wizard helps you properly install the necessary software programs for new Windows 98 applications.
Date/Time	This component helps you set the date and time, and the time zone for your personal computer.

Tool	Description
Desktop Themes	This component installs as a part of the Desktop Themes accessory. It is used to set up fancy colors, fonts, sounds, backgrounds, and mouse pointers for your PC.
Display	This component prompts you with the Display Properties dialog, where you configure such features as the monitor, screen saver, Active Desktop, and color schemes.
Fonts	This feature is used to add, change, or delete screen and printer fonts within the Windows 98 operating system.
Game Controllers	This feature is used to configure joysticks, steering wheels, and so forth, for use with Windows 98-compliant software.
Internet	This feature is used to configure the Internet Explorer Web browser.
Keyboard	This feature is used to configure the language, click blink, and the character speed rate of the PC keyboard for use with the Windows 98 operating system.
Mail	This function is used to control the property settings of the Inbox, including email, Exchange mail, and personal address folders.
Modems	This feature is used to confirm modem settings, as well as to perform basic diagnostic checks on your installed modems.
Mouse	This feature is used to modify the manner in which the attached PC mouse works, including its pointer attributes.
MS DTC	This icon is used to modify the transactional DTC client software configuration that was created for use with the Windows 98 Personal Web Server.

Tool	Description
Multimedia	This feature is used to modify the manner in which the attached audio, video, MIDI, CD music, and other multimedia devices map through the PC system.
Network	This Windows 98 component is required for the configuration of any networking function, including peer-to-peer, Dial-Up Networking, and for connecting a Windows 98 PC to the Internet, to a NetWare, Windows NT, or to a Banyan Vines system.
32-bit ODBC	This Microsoft Office component, which is installed as part of the MS Office software, might also appear in the Control Panel because of other installed 32-bit computer applications that require Open Database Connectivity (ODBC) features.
Passwords	This component can be used to configure Windows 98 passwords, some network passwords, Windows 98 Remote Administration, and User Profiles.
Power Management	This component is best used with corporate and/or mobile computers, in that Power Management modes are configurable for hard drives, monitors, and the Windows 98 computer system as a whole. For the home user, this component is probably best left off, because it might be rather annoying.
Printers	This Control Panel function can be used to configure Windows 98 printers. This feature operates in the same manner as the Printers feature that appears in the Start menu.
Regional Settings	This component controls the localization of the Windows 98 operating system, including the system language; time, dates, and currency formats; and the number and calendar types.
Sounds	This Control Panel option is used to configure the Windows 98 system event sounds.

Tool	Description
System	This option is used to configure full system components such as hardware devices, hardware startup profiles, system performance, cache sizes, and to view system information including IRQs, I/O ports, DMA Channels, and memory addresses.
Telephony	This feature permits you to predefine calling cards, and to configure telephony software drivers and Dial-Up Networking options.
Users	This feature is used to set up a PC for use with multiple users. It has a wizard feature that walks you step-by-step through its installation process.
Accessibility Options	This feature is used to modify Windows 98 for users with vision, hearing, and/or dexterity impairments.

DATE/TIME

Windows 98 keeps track of the system date and time for the computer. It is easy to view the date by hovering your mouse pointer over the time display, which appears on the right side of the taskbar.

Set Date/Time

1. Double-click the time display on the taskbar to open the **Date/Time Properties** dialog.
2. To change the date—for example, to January 1, 2000—click **1** in the calendar display, select **January** from the **Month** drop-down list, and click the up- or down-arrow button next to the **Year** text box to change the year to 2000.
3. To change the time, click the up- or down-arrow button beneath the clock.
4. To change the time zone, first click the **Time Zone** tab to open that screen.
5. If your time zone uses Daylight Savings Time, click the **Automatically adjust clock for daylight saving changes** check box. Windows 98 automatically updates twice a year to reflect daylight savings time changes. To change the time zone itself, click the down-arrow button near the top of the tab and select another time zone from the drop-down list. When you are satisfied with your selection, click once on the [OK] button.

> **NOTE**
> Notice the parenthetical items containing the initials GMT that appear in every Time Zone entry. GMT stands for Greenwich Mean Time, and the numeral following it (if any) indicates how many hours that time zone is ahead of or behind Greenwich Mean Time.

DESKTOP

The Windows 98 Desktop is the primary screen from which all activities originate; it is the screen that you see when you first start Windows 98. This screen typically contains a series of icons—including My Computer, Network Neighborhood, and the Recycle Bin—as well as a Channel bar that enables you to easily reach Internet content. The desktop can also be enabled as the Windows 98 Active Desktop.

See Also Active Desktop

DESKTOP THEMES

Desktop Themes, which are built into Windows 98, enable you to easily change your desktop background (also known as *wallpaper*), screen saver, sound events, mouse pointer graphics, system colors, desktop icon graphics, and system display fonts. Microsoft is continually releasing several additional variations to these Desktop Themes onto its Windows 98 Update and Windows Update Web sites, as well as providing several others in its Windows 98 add-on product known as Microsoft Plus! 98.

Use Desktop Themes

1. Click the **Start** button, choose **Settings**, and then choose **Control Panel**. This causes the Windows 98 Control Panel window to appear.

2. In the **Control Panel** window, double-click on the **Desktop Themes** icon. The **Desktop Themes** screen will appear with all the check boxes in the **Settings** section grayed out. This indicates that you cannot change any of the current theme's settings.

3. To switch to a different theme, click the down-arrow button to the right of the **Theme** text box, and select a new theme from the available list.

4. A preview of the selected theme is shown in the main portion of the screen. Notice that the check boxes in the **Settings** section are no longer grayed out. Uncheck any of the settings to see how the preview changes.

5. After you are satisfied with the theme you have chosen and any modifications you have made, click the **OK** button once to save any changes.

DIAL-UP NETWORKING

The Dial-Up Networking feature of Windows 98 permits you to connect to a remote network via a modem. This section focuses on connectivity for the mobile user, such as connecting to the Internet or your corporate network, using the Windows 98 technology known as Dial-Up Networking.

Configure Dial-Up Networking

1. Click the [Start] button, choose **Programs**, **Accessories**, **Communications**, and finally the **Dial-Up Networking** menu selection.

2. Double-click the **Make New Connection** icon in the **Dial-Up Networking** window to start the Make New Connection Wizard. This wizard will walk you through the steps of creating a Dial-Up Networking connection.

3. Type a name for the new connection in the text box at the top of the wizard's first screen (for example, you might want to leave the **Name** as the default, **My Connection**).

4. Select a modem device from the **Select a device** drop-down list (click the down-arrow button next to the text box to view the list). The default modem will typically be the one you want to use unless you have multiple modems connected to your PC. When you are satisfied with your selections, click the [Next >] button to continue.

5. In the next window, type the telephone number of the computer to which you will be connecting (this computer will typically belong to your Internet service provider). Be sure to select the correct country code (typically, it will be 1, which represents the United States of America). Click the [Next >] button to continue.

6. Click on the [Finish] button in the wizard's final screen, and you will return to the Dial-Up Networking window.

7. Notice that the connection you created using the wizard now appears in the Dial-Up Networking window.

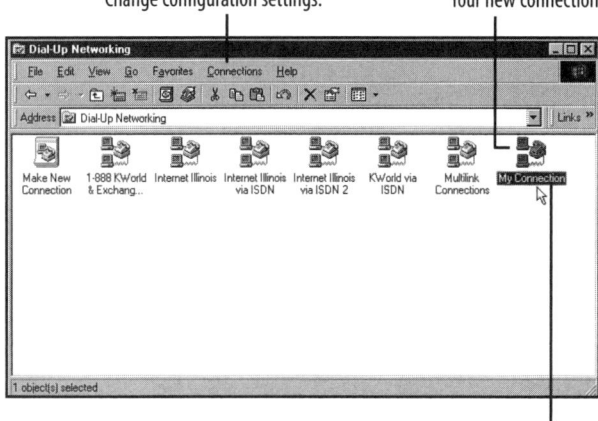

Change configuration settings.   Your new connection

Right-click to access Properties.

Check Dial-Up Networking Connections

1. Right-click the newly created **My Connection** icon and choose **Properties** from the ensuing shortcut menu.

> **NOTE**
> You can make changes to the telephone number and the modem selection in the **General** tab of the **My Connection** dialog. However, if you remember, you just entered this information while using the Make New Connection Wizard, so it should still be correct.

2. Click the **Server Types** tab whose default settings are typically adequate for most non-Internet connections. However, if you seek to connect to an Internet service provider (ISP), you will need to make a few changes.
3. Because the Internet supports only the use of TCP/IP, uncheck the **NetBEUI** and **IPX/SPX Compatible** check boxes in the **Allowed network protocols** section of the **Server Types** tab, which will free up some of your system resources.

4. To configure your TCP/IP connection, click the [TCP/IP Settings...] button to open the TCP/IP Settings dialog.

> **NOTE**
>
> Most likely, the only settings your ISP will ask you to change are the primary and secondary DNS (Domain Name Server) numbers. To do so, select the **Specify name server addresses** radio button and type the appropriate primary DNS, secondary DNS, primary WINS, and secondary WINS (WINS settings are typically used only for corporate network connectivity, as it is extremely unlikely that an ISP will require this technology). A typical address might be 10.10.5.100. The information that goes into these address boxes will be provided by your Internet service provider (or local system administrator, should you be doing this at work).

5. Click [OK] to return to the Server Types tab of the My Connection dialog.

> **TIP**
>
> DNS addresses represent the TCP/IP address for that particular DNS server. When you connect to the Internet via your local ISP, all you usually need is that ISP's DNS addressing scheme. This usually comes in the form of the primary and the secondary DNS addresses.

6. If you want to combine the transmission power of more than one modem at a time with your PC, click once on the **Multilink** tab to access that the screen. (Your ISP or corporate network must permit you to log in multiple times with the same User ID in order for Multilink to work.)

7. Click once on the **Use additional devices** radio button, and then click the [Add...] button to place additional modems in the Multilink tab.

> **NOTE**
>
> Remember that you must have a distinctly separate telephone line for each modem placed in the Multilink tab; a party line will not work for this purpose.

8. To accept all the changes that you made in the My Connection dialog and return to the Dial-Up Networking window, click once on the OK button. Close the Dial-Up Networking window by clicking the × button that appears in the upper-right corner.

DIAL-UP SERVER

The Windows 98 Dial-Up Server feature enables you to use your own PC as a server to which other computers can dial up for remote access. This feature cannot be configured unless you have installed the proper files for the Dial-Up Networking function (refer to the "Add/Remove Programs" section for information about installing components, and refer to the "Dial-Up Networking" section for more information about that feature).

Configure Dial-Up Server

1. Click the Start button, choose **Programs**, **Accessories**, **Communications**, and finally select the **Dial-Up Networking** menu selection.

2. Click once on the **Connections** menu option and then select the **Dial-Up Server** menu selection.

3. This screen enables you to configure the service so that you can permit others to dial into your PC. Select the **Allow caller access** radio button. Then, click once on the Server Type... button to specify what type of dial-up connectivity is supported by your computer.

4. Because you are using Windows 98, select the **PPP: Internet, Windows NT Server, Windows 98** option from the **Type of Dial-Up Server** drop-down list in the **Server Types** window.

5. If the clients dialing in are not necessarily going to be using Windows 95, Windows 98, or Windows NT, uncheck the **Require encrypted password** check box because non-Windows clients might have difficulty transmitting an encrypted password.

> **NOTE**
> The Enable Software Compression option should be left as is (*selected*), unless you are sure that your modem's hardware functions better (that is, it can transmit more data in the same period of time) than the software compression that is built into Windows 98.

6. Click once on the OK button in the Server Types dialog and then again in the Dial-Up Server dialog to complete the configuration process.
7. Click once on the **Allow caller access** radio button to permit others to dial into your PC via this technology. If you click once on the **Change Password** button, then you can set a predefined password that others must use when they are connecting to your computer.
8. Click once on the OK button to complete the configuration process.

See Also Dial-Up Networking

DIRECT CABLE CONNECTION

The Direct Cable Connection feature is useful if you want to exchange files between two computers, but you do not want to set up a network. The reason for this is that you will use a single cable to directly connect the two PCs across which your files can be copied. You will need a special cable, such as the one provided with LapLink (a third-party hardware/software data transfer company).

Configure Direct Cable Connection

1. Click the Start button, and choose **Programs**, **Accessories**, **Communications**, and finally click on the **Direct Cable Connection** menu selection.

2. The Direct Cable Connection Wizard begins. In the first screen, you must specify whether you are currently using the **Host** computer or the **Guest** computer. After you make your selection click once on the `Next >` button to continue.

> **NOTE**
>
> The *host* computer contains the resources that you want to access, whereas the *guest* computer is the system that will be performing the accessing. However, it is important to note that regardless of the connection type, a guest computer can still copy its own files to the host computer. This means that a guest computer can *act* like a host computer even though it is the guest.

3. In the next screen, you will actually start the connection process, which means that you must have a serial or parallel cable to connect the two computers. To do this, highlight the connection method—parallel or serial—along with the port on which the connection will be made.

> **NOTE**
>
> A *parallel cable* connects into the parallel port of each computer. This cable will closely resemble a standard parallel printer cable (except that its ends will typically fit on either a 9-pin or a 25-pin serial connection), and transfers data much faster than a serial cable could (average transmission rate is roughly three times faster over a parallel cable than a serial one).
>
> A *serial cable* is one that connects into a serial port of each computer. It can be connected to the COM1: port on the guest side, while using the COM2: port on the host side. The serial cable will closely resemble a standard modem cable and provides a relatively slow transmission rate (especially when compared to that of a parallel cable).

4. Click once on the `Next >` button to access the next screen, whose dialog informs you that you have successfully configured the guest computer. Click once on the `Finish` button to continue the process.

5. Before a Direct Cable Connection can be made, you must run the same wizard process on the other computer and configure it as the host computer (select the **Host** option in step 2).

6. After you complete the steps in the wizard, click once on the `Finish` button.

> **NOTE**
>
> After the connection is complete and you have transferred all the files/data that you want, click on the ⊠ button to terminate the Direct Cable Connection. Remember that once you click on the ⊠ button, you can no longer use that Direct Cable Connection session.

DISK CLEANUP

The Disk Cleanup function is an automated way for Windows 98 to delete extraneous files, such as temporary Internet files, other temporary files, downloaded ActiveX and Java program applets, documents in the Recycle Bin, temporary Windows 98 files, and the removal of the Windows 98 Uninstall information (provided you have not already performed the cleanup of this last option at least once).

Use Disk Cleanup

1. Click the `Start` button, choose **Programs**, **Accessories**, **System Tools**, and finally click on the **Disk Cleanup**. The first Disk Cleanup dialog shows you how far Windows 98 has progressed while it determines how much hard disk space the Disk Cleanup program can save.

2. On the **Disk Cleanup** tab, place a check mark next to the types of files you want removed, and then click once on the `OK` button to continue.

> **TIP**
>
> One of the more difficult tasks is trying to remember exactly what files one has downloaded or deleted. This is where the `View Files` button comes into play. Clicking once on this button presents you with a listing of which files are contained within the bin that your mouse pointer is presently highlighting. A single click on the `View Files` button will show you not only what the Temporary Internet Files are, but also provide you with an opportunity to delete them. The `View Files` button is only present for use with Temporary Internet Files, Downloaded Program Files, and the Recycle Bin.

> **NOTE**
>
> If you use the Internet as much as I do (which is about 45-60 minutes daily), the **Temporary Internet Files** entry will probably contain most of the disk-cleanup opportunities.

3. If the **Total space to be cleaned** section of the **Disk Cleanup** tab reads 0 MB, click once on the **More Options** tab to continue.

> **CAUTION**
>
> Be very careful about deleting files that you do not understand, nor have a clear idea as to whether or not you (or your computer) would miss having these files around. In the case of Recycle Bin and Temporary Internet Files, this warning might not be applicable. However, with the others, please think about what you are doing before performing the Clean Up process. It is always better to be safe, rather than sorry when it comes to your PC.

4. Click the `Clean up...` button in the Windows components area to open the **Windows Setup** tab of the Add/Remove Programs Properties dialog. You can now safely delete Windows 98 options.

5. After you have made your selections, click once on the `OK` button to process the changes. This will maximize the Disk Clean Up screen.

6. Click the [Clean up..] button in the **Installed programs** area to open the **Install/Uninstall** tab of the Add/Remove Programs Properties dialog. You can now safely delete any third-party applications that you do not require by selecting them in the list and clicking the [Add/Remove Programs] button.

7. When you are through deleting/removing programs, click once on the [OK] button to exit the dialog. This will then return you back to the Disk Clean Up window.

> **CAUTION**
>
> It is strongly recommended that you do not remove applications you do not recognize, unless you are the only user of the PC and it is a computer for home use. Deleting things you do not understand usually leads to computing oblivion.

See Also Add/Remove Programs

DISK DEFRAGMENTER

The Windows 98 Disk Defragmenter enables you to rearrange files on you hard drive so that software programs can find files faster. This, in turn, will help applications run faster. Another plus of the Disk Defragmenter is that it automatically rearranges the free disk space on your hard drive, which might give you more free space to work with.

Disk Defragmenter's help text states that you can run other programs while using Disk Defragmenter. Although this might technically be a true statement, it is strongly recommended that you run the Disk Defragmenter program by itself because it greatly affects the performance of other running programs. Even worse, running other programs, such as word processors, alongside Disk Defragmenter can cause it to continually lose its place and restart. This is because word processors and other programs write to the hard drive that Defragmenter is trying to defragment. It is possible, then, to use Disk Defragmenter throughout the course of an entire day and never finish the process, while dramatically slowing the processing power of your PC.

Even when other applications are not running, Defragmenter can take a long time to complete. Do not fret if it takes several hours to run the disk defragmenter utility, especially if it has been a long time since you last ran this utility. You might want to run Defragmenter during a down time, such as during lunch, just as you are leaving work (letting it run overnight while you are out of the office), or just before you go to bed. One way to avoid some of the headache you are bound for is to use the Scheduled Tasks Manager component of Windows 98. Please refer to that section of this book for further details on how to do this.

Run Disk Defragmenter

1. Click the [Start] button, choose the **Programs** menu option, followed by **Accessories**, **System Tools**, and then **Disk Defragmenter**.

2. Select the drive you want to defragment from the drop-down list in the Select Drive dialog, and then click once on the [Settings...] button to continue.

3. Use the Disk Defragmenter Settings dialog to configure the disk defragmentation process for every defragmentation operation or for only the current one. It is recommended that you check both options in the **When defragmenting my hard drive** section (note, however, that checking these options slows the defragmentation process) and that you use these options every time you defragment your hard drive. After you make your selections, click once on the [OK] button to start the Defragmenter application.

4. During the defragmentation process, you will see a dialog containing a Progress bar. If you want to end the defragmentation process before its completion, click the [Stop] button.

> **NOTE**
>
> Keep in mind that not all the defragmentation has been completed if you stop it before its natural ending. This means that if you stop it after it is 55 percent done, it might not restart at the 56 percent location. Rather, it will start over (granted, it may get to the 56 percent location faster, but nothing is guaranteed under Windows 98 in this area).

5. You will then see a completion box. Click once on the **Yes** button and the program will end automatically.

DISPLAY OPTIONS

Windows 98 display options enable you to change how your computer desktop is displayed, as well as to manipulate the various screen fonts and colors that will be present throughout the many Windows applications on your PC.

Change Display Options

1. Right-click a blank portion of the desktop and choose the **Properties** option from the shortcut menu.

2. The Display Properties dialog appears with the Background tab selected by default. You can specify an HTML document or picture to use as a background for your desktop.

> **NOTE**
>
> The tabs in your Display Properties screen might differ slightly from the standard ones that come with the Windows 98 operating system. The core tabs—that you will have on your machine—are Background, Screen Saver, Appearance, Effects, Settings, and Web. However, chances are that your computer will have a vendor-specific tab as well.

3. Click the **Screen Saver** tab so that you can choose a screen saver to be displayed on your machine, establish how long your computer must be idle before the screen-saver image is displayed, and, if desired, set a password

for returning to your work once the screen saver has been displayed.

> **NOTE**
>
> The original purpose of screen savers was to prevent a phenomenon known as *burn-in*, in which a faint image of the contents of your screen remained present even after you turned off your computer. Although people with older monitors still use screen savers for this purpose, screen savers are now used primarily for entertainment value.

4. The Screen Saver tab also enables you to configure your monitor's energy-saving features. To change these settings click the `Settings...` button, make your choices in that tab's screen and click once on the `OK` button to return to the Display Properties dialog.

> **NOTE**
>
> If the `Settings...` button is grayed out, that indicates that your monitor does support energy-saving features.

5. To modify the PC colors, fonts, and general appearance, click the **Appearance** tab. Click once on the down-arrow button to the right of the **Scheme** text box to view the **Scheme** drop-down list. Select the scheme you want from the list; a preview of the scheme will appear in the display window above the **Scheme** text box.

6. Click once on the **Effects** tab to access that screen's contents. Here you can change the icons associated with various Windows 98 features. Select the icon you want to change in the **Desktop icons** area, and then click the `Change Icon...` button.

7. This next screen prompts you for the name of a file that contains Windows-compatible icon graphics. After you have entered the filename, press the `↵Enter` key (on your computer's keyboard) and any available icons will appear in the box.

8. Click once on the [OK] button to return to the **Effects** tab of the Display Properties dialog, after you have made your selection.
9. If you want to hide icons when using the Active Desktop feature of Windows 98, click once on the **Hide icons when the desktop is viewed as a Web page** check box in the **Effects** tab.
10. Alter the manner in which icons and the Windows 98 Desktop appear to users by checking or unchecking features in the **Visual effects** section. Play around with these options to find the effects that please you most.
11. Click the **Web** tab to use the features of the Web from Windows 98, you must first activate the Active Desktop. Do so by checking the **View my Active Desktop as a Web page** check box.
12. You can now add HTML and Web-related content (such as JPEG and GIF graphics, as well as animated GIF files). To add a file, click once on the [New] button and pick a file from your local hard drive.
13. Click once on the **Settings** tab to access the next screen, which enables you to alter the resolution of your monitor as well as to set the number of colors available for use.

> **NOTE**
> The lower the screen resolution (for example, 640×480), the larger the characters and graphics will appear to be. If you were to choose a higher resolution (such as 800×600), the screen characters and graphics would appear to be smaller.

> **NOTE**
> If, in the **Colors** area, you specify that a large number of colors be used, as is the case when you select **High Color (16 bit)**, it might have a negative impact on your system's overall performance.

14. To accept your changes in the Display Properties dialog and return to the desktop, click once on the [OK] button.

DOCUMENT TEMPLATES

A *document template* is a file that enables you to easily create and automatically reuse a certain type of document for a specific Windows 98 application. Windows 98 comes with several pre-defined templates for use, including a Microsoft HTML Document version 4.0, a Notepad text file, Bitmap Images (used with Microsoft Paint), WordPad files, new Briefcases (in addition to the default one), and a shortcut to the My Documents folder that sits on the Windows 98 Desktop. Please keep in mind that these templates create essentially blank or empty documents for the above applications.

If you create your own document templates, then you will be able to customize the starting point for document creation. For instance, the Microsoft Word template just gives you a blank document. However, if you made your own template within Microsoft Word (a .DOT file) and saved it into the Document Templates folder for Microsoft Office (usually C:\Program Files\Microsoft Office\Templates), then you could apply this template to your Microsoft Word document. This becomes useful when creating the same types of documents repeatedly; such as office memos that have a standard letterhead look with the appropriate wording.

Use Predefined Document Template

1. Right-click a blank portion of the desktop, choose the **New** menu option from the pop-up shortcut menu, and then choose the **Microsoft Word Document** menu selection.
2. An empty version of a Word document is placed on the Windows 98 Desktop. Rename the document or use it as is by double-clicking on it to open it (this only

works, provided that you have an installed version of Microsoft Word on your computer).

DRIVESPACE

DriveSpace enables you to expand the size of your hard drive artificially, which allows you to save more information on that hard drive, even though its physical size has not changed. Maybe you will want to think of DriveSpace as a bit like magic. It uses a different storage algorithm for mapping bytes of information to a drive, than does the normal storage process. However, it is just as safe not to use DriveSpace on your drive.

> **NOTE**
> DriveSpace 3 is not compatible with a FAT32-formatted hard drive, so if you are using FAT32, this application is not for you. When you run out of space on FAT32, you will need to purchase another hard drive.

Run DriveSpace

1. Click the **Start** button, choose **Programs, Accessories, System Tools**, and then select the **DriveSpace Connection** menu selection.
2. The DriveSpace 3 window opens. To compress a drive, click the **Drive** menu and then choose the **Compress** option.
3. This starts the **Compression** Wizard. Carefully follow each step to complete the process.
4. After you complete the wizard, you will have considerably more free hard drive space as well as two hard drives (one is a physical drive and the other is the logical drive).

NOTE

This new "logical" drive is actually your C: drive, whereas the physical hard drive becomes known as another drive letter (probably H:, but could be as low as D: in the alphabet). Continue to use your C: drive just as you have in the past, and try not to place any files or applications on your new (probably H:) drive. The reason you do not want to put files on the new H: drive is that you would actually be lowering the amount of free space that you had available on the C: drive. Sounds confusing? It is. Basically, your C: drive is created from this new H: drive, so if you take away space on H:, then you will have even less space available on the C: drive.

Compress Free Space

1. Click the **Advanced** menu option and then choose the **Create Empty** option.

2. This starts the **Compression** Wizard. Again, follow each of the steps carefully to complete the process. Upon completion, you will have approximately double the free hard drive space as you did before, as well as the two hard drives (one is a physical drive and the other is the logical drive).

NOTE

For the nonbelievers in the crowd: Yes, DriveSpace is a safe application that will not corrupt your data at whim. However, keep in mind that DriveSpace can create too much overhead on slower systems, which then results in your system's I/O slowing way down. Unless sufficient disk space is available, DriveSpace cannot be removed, something else that can get a novice user into a lot of trouble. You would be much better off by using FAT32, though DriveSpace can provide more available hard disk space. Microsoft has let its DriveSpace technology stagnate because hard disks these days are much larger than when Microsoft first introduced DriveSpace.

DVD PLAYER

The Digital Versatile Disc (DVD) Player uses a revolutionary new format for those discs that so closely resemble ordinary CD-ROMs. DVD discs look and act just like CDs, except that they can store quite a bit more data (roughly 2,600MB, on DVD versus 640MB on CD). In addition, as the DVD standards evolve, this storage level is expected to increase immensely (at least double). Both DVD discs and CDs can be read by the DVD-ROM drive, and the drive will function just as your old CD-ROM drive did.

The most noticeable difference to you will be in the operation of a DVD-ROM drive. Because a DVD disc can store not only audio and computer data, but video as well, you must have special hardware and software to access this video portion. The hardware is called an MPEG decoder card (MPEG stands for: Motion Pictures Expert Group). The DVD software required is the DVD Player that is built into Windows 98.

To start the DVD Player, click once on the [Start] button, then choose **Programs**, **Accessories**, **Entertainment**, and finally the **DVD Player**.

Because most DVD-ROM players require specialized software specific to their decoder card, the DVD software support built into Windows 98 might not be sufficient for your DVD-ROM drive (it is not for either Gateway 2000 computers or Toshiba laptops, and I suspect not for most computer systems out there). For this reason, you are generally better off using the custom DVD software that came with your computer's DVD-ROM drive than you would be using the Windows 98 DVD Player software.

EMAIL

Windows 98 contains very good electronic mail (email) and electronic newsgroup (news) software-accessing tools, which are built directly into the Windows 98 operating system. Outlook Express could easily survive on its own as a standalone email and newsgroup product. HOWEVER, MICROSOFT FIRST chose to integrate it into its Internet Explorer Web browser product (for use with Windows 95), and then Microsoft completely integrated it into the Windows 98 operating system.

Before you start using either of these applications, you will want to make sure that you have obtained all the latest and greatest updates to the Microsoft Outlook Express application. Presently these are available on the Windows 98 Windows Update Web site (refer to the section on "Windows Update" if you do not know how to do this on your own) at the following URL:

    http://windowsupdate.microsoft.com/.

> **NOTE**
> It is strongly recommended that you at least review the sections on Outlook Express and Internet Explorer before you begin using either of these tools. The reasoning for this is that you may pick up a few tips or tricks that will make your Internet surfing/email experience a bit more pleasant your first time out there.

See Also Internet Explorer, Outlook Express

EASTER EGG

The incredibly intelligent software developers that Microsoft Corporation has employed over the years to create and deploy their repertoire of software products are also practical jokers of sorts. In nearly every released product, these development teams have left their own personalized trademarks within each product. These examples have come in many forms, from the flight simulator in Microsoft

Excel 97, to the "killer W" inside the Microsoft Word 2.0 package, to the musically adept Windows 95 credits listing. These secret features are known throughout the computing industry as *Easter Eggs*. The Windows 98 Easter Egg is essentially a credit listing to all those persons who participated in the creation of this amazing new operating system from Microsoft.

Access to the Windows 98 Easter Egg is no different in concept than access to the others that have come before it. Although the hoops that one needs to jump through to get the Easter Egg to appear do require a bit of mouse agility and geographic knowledge.

Find Easter Egg

1. Double-click the time display on the taskbar to open the **Date/Time Properties** dialog. After it appears, click once on the **Time Zone** tab.

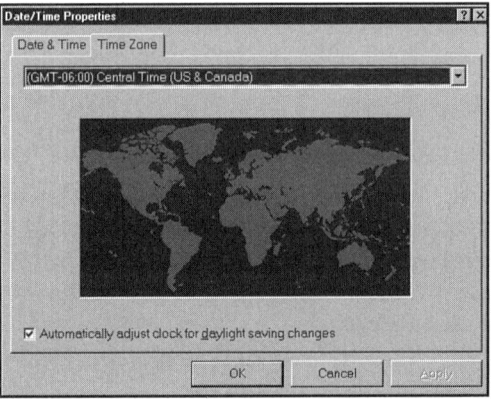

2. Place your mouse pointer over Memphis, Egypt (it is right by the Red Sea, between the main part of Egypt and the Sinai peninsula). While holding down the Ctrl key, click and hold the left mouse button and drag the mouse pointer over to Memphis, Tennessee (if you do not know where this is, just ask Elvis).

3. Let go of first the mouse button and then the Ctrl key (you do need to perform these tasks in this order).

4. Repeat steps 2 and 3, but this time you will go from Memphis, Tennessee to Redmond, Washington (Redmond, for you non-Microsofties, is located just to the east of Seattle).

Successful completion of these steps results in the Windows 98 credits rolling across your computer screen.

> **NOTE**
> Do not be alarmed if it takes you a few dozen attempts to get this Easter Egg to work.

EMERGENCY STARTUP DISK

There are times when you need to perform a clean restart of your computer directly from a floppy disk. This might be because you want to eliminate a virus from your computer. (The virus detection packages usually cannot be installed onto an infected PC, so a clean startup will keep the virus from loading itself into memory). It might also be because your Windows 98 installation is failing and you want to troubleshoot its failures.

The term *Emergency boot disk* is the informal name for the Windows 98 Startup Disk. The purpose of the Startup Disk is to help you get back into your computer should the Windows 98 operating system fail for any reason. The Startup Disk contains specialized boot files that will start up the operating system from a single floppy disk and then attempt to restore operations to your computer. Use of the Startup Disk should be a last resort, because it is possible that it will overwrite some critical system information possibly forcing you to reinstall one or more of your applications.

A Windows 98 Startup Disk enables you to perform a clean startup of your computer system. Creating the Startup Disk requires a single high-density 3 1/2-inch floppy disk and about five minutes of your time. The facility to create this disk comes with Windows 98, so there is nothing extra you have to buy or download from the Internet. You will also need to have your Windows 98 CD-ROM handy during the creation process.

The easiest time to create a Startup Disk is during the installation of Windows 98. If you recall, during the installation process you were prompted to insert a floppy disk into your floppy drive for precisely this reason. However, if you are reviewing this topic, you probably skipped on making a Startup Disk at that time.

Create Startup Disk

1. Access the **Add/Remove Programs** icon by double-clicking it in the Windows 98 Control Panel.
2. After the Add/Remove Programs dialog appears, click the **Startup Disk** tab to access its screen.
3. To create the Startup Disk, insert your blank (formatted) floppy disk into your computer's A:\ drive and then click once on the `Create Disk...` button.
4. A pop-up message box will appear asking you to insert your Windows 98 CD-ROM before continuing. Do this and then click the `OK` button once to continue.
5. A status bar appears showing how the creation operation is progressing. Somewhere around the 20-percent complete mark, it will prompt you to place a formatted floppy disk into your computer's A:\ drive. Because you have already done this (in step 3), click once on the `OK` button to continue.

> **NOTE**
> The disk creation process continues automatically, and after it is complete, you will see just the screen you started with. Windows 98 does not give you any indication that the Startup Disk creation process finished, much less whether it did so successfully. After the progress bar disappears, you are supposed to know intuitively that the process is complete.

6. Test the Startup Disk that you made by restarting your computer with the disk still in the floppy drive. If your system starts up, it works (you will see a Windows 98 Menu appear at the MS-DOS prompt). Make the selection you want to continue the boot process.
7. If the computer not start up, repeat the Startup Disk creation process.

See Also Add/Remove Programs

FAT32 CONVERTER

The FAT32 converter is a hard-disk, file-storage format designed especially for drives with more than 512MB of space. Because FAT32 is a new 32-bit file allocation table format, it does not support dual startup functionality with the other Windows operating systems available today. If you are using a relatively small hard drive (less than 512MB total), you cannot use FAT32, so you may want to consider disk compression if you are still looking to obtain more space on your existing hard drives.

Run Drive Converter

1. Click once on the [Start] button, then choose **Programs**, **Accessories**, **System Tools**, and then click once on the **Drive Converter (FAT32)** menu selection.

2. This starts the **Drive Converter (FAT32)** Wizard. If you want to learn more about the whole drive converting process, click once on the [Details] button. To continue, click once on the [Next >] button.

3. First click once on the hard drive that you want upgraded to the FAT32 format, and then click once on the [Next >] button to continue the process.

> **NOTE**
>
> A message box may appear that tells you to be careful if you have a computer that possesses the capability to hibernate, such as an IBM ThinkPad laptop. The reason for this is that your computer might lose data if it does go into a hibernation or suspend mode.

4. When you are certain that your computer's hibernation features (if there are any) are disabled, click once on the [OK] button to continue.

5. The Drive Converter Wizard checks your PC to see whether you have any virus protection applications enabled because these types of programs may conflict

with the drive conversion process. Click once on the `Next>` button to continue the process.

6. You are prompted to back up your system's files (never a bad idea). Clicking once on the `Backup` button will start the Windows 98 Backup utility that helps you through the backup process. Click once on the `Next>` button to continue the process.

> **CAUTION**
>
> To perform the conversion process, Windows 98 will be restarted in its MS-DOS mode where the conversion process actually takes place. Be forewarned, though, that the entire process may take several hours to complete and cannot be interrupted for any reason whatsoever. In fact, if you attempt to restart or otherwise halt the process, you will more than likely corrupt your system that includes the corruption of data.

7. After the conversion process is complete, the Drive Converter tool restarts your PC, at which time the process will be complete.

FAVORITES

Windows 98 Favorites are *hyperlinks* to Internet/intranet Web sites. You do not necessarily have to save your favorite sites in Internet Explorer's **Favorites** list (which is the same as the **Favorites** list found under the **Favorites** option in the **Start** menu). For example, you can store shortcuts (which are essentially Favorites) directly on your Windows 98 active desktop that will quickly take you to your favorite location on the Web. If you double-click such a link, Windows 98 will start its default Web browser and then take you to the appropriate Internet site. If you forget to connect to the Internet before executing a **Favorites** link, an error message box will appear telling you that it cannot find the Web site you seek.

Use Favorites List

1. Click the [Start] button and then choose **Favorites**.
2. Click any of the entries in the **Favorites** menu (you might need to click a folder or two to reach the Web site you want to visit) to start your default Web browser. The default Web browser will probably be Microsoft Internet Explorer, as it is the one integrated into the Windows 98 operating system. The browser automatically opens the file, folder, or Web site that you have selected.

> **TIP**
> Usually in folks'"Favorites" listings, most of what you see are folders. To actually access a Favorite, you first must click on any of the Favorite folders, and then on the actual Favorite, such as one that might be in your United States Government folder (for example, the Library of Congress, US Patent Office, and the CIA Web sites).

See Also Shortcuts

Organize Favorites into Folders

1. To add a new site to your **Favorites** list, first visit the site you want to add.
2. Click once on the **Favorites** menu option and then select the **Add to Favorites** menu selection.
3. This will open the Add Favorite dialog.
4. There is a [Create in >>] button on this screen that enables you to add a new Favorite into a folder (existing or you can make a new one) within the Windows 98 Favorites section. Clicking on this button expands this same dialog into a larger one that shows the folder structure of your current Favorites area.
5. Scrolling down your existing Favorites structure, you need to select your target folder for the Favorite you want to add. Click on that folder with the left mouse button first and then click on the [OK] button to insert this new Web site's location into your **Favorites** section.

6. Click again on the **Favorites** menu option to confirm that the **Favorite** has been added as desired.
7. To organize sites into folders, click the **Favorites** menu item and select **Organize** Favorites. The Organize Favorites screen appears.

> **NOTE**
>
> From the Organize Favorites screen you can move, rename, delete, and/or open an existing Favorite. It is suggested that you use the standard file management techniques for your Windows 98 Favorites, just as you do for the rest of your computer. For example, the Favorites folder on my home computer contains over 1,300 Favorite links. If all of those links were dumped into a single folder, it would be quite unmanageable for anyone to use.

FILE MANAGEMENT

Files are the software creations that make all things possible in PC computing today. Every folder, word processing document, software application, and operating system feature is actually nothing more than a file. Files come with the Windows 98 operating system (thousands of them, actually), with each software application that you load on your PC, and even more are created by these same applications (in the form of word processing documents, spreadsheets, and the like). What one does with the files on their PC is the important part.

File management is one of the most important functions that you, the user, are responsible for in regards to the use of your computer. It is strongly recommended that you devise some scheme with which to organize the file structure for storing files on your computer. Microsoft has given you a starting point for this in the realm of its folder labeled "Program Files." This folder is found in the Windows 98 directory structure directly off the root directory (C:\Program Files) and contains most of the applications that are installed on your computer.

To make things work easier, it is suggested that you create a folder hierarchy that will enable you to save your own files in a manner that will make it easier to locate for future use. For example, if you have a folder called DATA with a series of subfolders named after the respective application that created these folders' contents, it would be easy to find, use, modify, and/or back up these files as necessary. This file structure might look like that found in the following arrangement:

C:\DATA

C:\DATA\EXCEL

C:\DATA\POWERPOINT

C:\DATA\PUBLISHER

C:\DATA\QUICKEN

C:\DATA\WORD

Files can be copied, or swapped, between two computers with the Direct Cable Connection feature of Windows 98 (refer to that section of this book, if you need more information on using this tool). After the two computers are connected, it is simply a matter of using the drag-and-drop method of moving files. (See "Move Files," which appears later in this section.) The only difference is that although you are dragging and dropping a file between the two computers, you are actually leaving the original file on the first computer so this is a copy operation and not a move operation. Because the second computer will appear as a different disk drive within the My Computer folder, it will basically look like you are just moving/copying files between locations on your own PC.

Of course, you are probably wondering how you can get your existing files into the new structure that you might have just created. To do this, you need to either move or copy your existing files over to their new folders. Use the next few sections to perform these relatively simple computing tasks.

Copy Files

1. First, you must know which file you want to copy. (Suppose, for example, that you want to copy the Microsoft Word shortcut file.) To access the source file (that is, the one you want to copy), double-click on the **My Computer** icon to open the My Computer window.

2. Double-click the drive where the file that you want to copy exists. If in doubt, start with the C: drive; it is usually the primary (if not the only) hard drive in a PC. This will then open another Windows Explorer window, which you will use to maneuver your way over to the folder that holds the source file (in this case, the **Microsoft Office** folder).

3. The title bar of your screen will now probably read `C:\Program Files\Microsoft Office`. Find the file you want to copy—the shortcut for Microsoft Word.

4. Select this file by clicking it once with the left mouse button; then right-click the selected file and choose **Copy** from the shortcut menu. The file you have selected is copied to the Clipboard (refer to the section labeled "Clipboard" for more details).

5. Move to the place where you want to paste the copy of the file, such as the Windows 98 Desktop (you can reach this spot by minimizing or closing one or more of your open windows).

6. Right-click once on a blank portion of the desktop and choose **Paste** from the ensuing shortcut menu.

7. The Microsoft Word shortcut file is pasted to the desktop and will appear there right in front of your eyes.

Delete Files

1. First, you must know which file you want to delete. To access the source file (that is, the one you want to copy), double-click the **My Computer** icon to open the My Computer window.

2. Double-click the drive where the file that you want to delete exists. If in doubt, start with the C: drive.

3. When you find the file you want to delete, click on it once to select it.

4. Right-click the selected file and select **Delete** from the shortcut menu. This will remove the selected file from the window and move it into the Windows 98 Recycle Bin for later removal from your computer (review the section on the Windows 98 Recycle Bin for more details).

> **TIP**
>
> An easier way to delete a file is to first select it by clicking on it once, and then press the Del key on your keyboard.

5. Close the C: window and return to the desktop by closing or minimizing all open windows. Then double-click the **Recycle Bin** icon on your desktop.

6. Note that the deleted file now appears in the Recycle Bin.

7. To delete it permanently from your system, click once on the **Recycle Bin** with the right mouse button.

8. A pop-up menu appears, where you need to click once on the **Empty Recycle Bin** menu selection. A message box displays, prompting you as to whether or not you really want to delete the files in the bin. It will also give the precise name of the file to be deleted if there is just one file in the Recycle Bin, otherwise this message box will only tell you the total number of files to be deleted.

9. Click once on the **Yes** button to complete the deletion process. You will then be returned to the Windows 98 Desktop screen where you now see that the Recycle Bin is completely empty.

Move Files

1. Start the **Windows Explorer** tool by clicking once on the **Start** button, then choosing **Programs, Windows Explorer**.

2. The Explorer window opens. To find the file you seek, first find the folder where it resides. You might have to click a series of folders to reach the file you seek.
3. Click the file you want to move to select it.
4. Using the scrollbar in the left pane, scroll to the folder where you want the file to be moved. Hold down the left mouse button and drag the file to its new location. When the destination folder becomes highlighted, release the mouse button.

The file that you moved now resides in the folder that you last selected.

FILE ASSOCIATIONS

Sometimes when you install a new product, such as a word processor, it will alter the file associations that already exist on your PC. For example, documents with a .doc file extension (a.k.a., a file association) are originally associated with the Windows 98 WordPad tool. However, after you install the Microsoft Word word processor application, you will notice that any time you double-click on a .doc file the Microsoft Word application will automatically start with that file opened inside of Word, instead of being opened inside the old WordPad tool. This is because that file extension is being associated with another software application.

There are probably dozens, if not more, of file types configured on your Windows 98 PC. These file type configurations are better known as *File Associations*, which means that if you attempt to open a file directly, it will "call" the file type association to see which application is used to open this file. For example, if you double-click on a *.PPT file, the Microsoft PowerPoint application will start up and then open the file that you just double-clicked.

Change File Associations

1. Double-click the **My Computer** icon found on your Windows 98 Desktop.

2. Click once on the **View** menu option, and then choose **Folder Options**, **File Types**.

3. From this screen, you are able to add new file associations (types) and delete existing ones. The option you are most interested in is the modification of existing file types.

4. Locate the **Registered File Type** that you want to modify by scrolling down the screen.

5. Select this file type by clicking on it once. Then, to access that file type's associations, you need to click the [Edit] button, which takes you to the Edit File Type screen.

6. To modify an existing file type association, click once on the **Action** type shown in the box on the bottom half of the screen.

7. Click once on the [Edit] button to reveal the Editing Action for Type screen.

8. The **Application used to perform the action** option asks which program you want to use in association with this file type. You can use the [Browse..] button to determine the path and executable file that you want to use with this particular file type.

9. After you have made your changes and selections, click once on the [OK] button to save your changes to this file type and return to the Edit File Type window. If you want a new action to be associated with a particular file type, you can do so from here as well.

10. You can give your new action a name in the **Action** box (most actions are one word in length, such as Open, Close, Run, Edit), and then you need to enter the exact path and filename for the executable to be run.

11. After you have finished making your entries, click once on the [OK] button to save your changes and return to the Edit File Type window.

12. From there, click once on the `OK` button to exit the Folder Options screen and return to the My Computer window or from wherever you originally started this whole process (such as the Windows Explorer tool).
13. Close that window to finish.

FIND

The Find command under Windows 98 is greatly improved compared to older versions of Windows. Not only can you search for files, folders, and computers on your network, you can also search for friends on the Internet, and items in your address book.

There are two ways to find people: locally (that is, within your own PC's address book), or globally (that is, using one of the many Internet search engines to locate the person you seek).

Find Files and Folders on Your Computer

1. Click once on the `Start` button, and then choose **Find**. You will see the Find menu, which contains the various Find options.
2. Click the first item, **Files or Folders**, to open the Find: All Files screen (with the Name & Location tab displayed).
3. Type the name of the file you're looking for and its extension (.doc, .ppt, .xls, and so on) if you know it.
4. Select the drive in which the file resides (such as the C: drive) from the **Look in** drop-down list. Alternatively, type some text that the file contains in the **Containing text** text box.
5. To narrow a search, you can enter the date when the file was created, last modified, or last accessed. To do so, click the **Date** tab of the Find: All Files dialog.

> **NOTE**
>
> Although this screen will search by a series of days or dates, you should still enter either a filename or a text string on the **Previous** tab. Otherwise, you probably will not be able to locate the file that you are looking for because too many files are automatically modified or accessed by the operating system without you ever realizing it.

6. If you leave this screen at its default settings, **All files**, it instructs Windows 98 to search through all files from all dates, which does not exactly take advantage of the functions of this screen. Instead, click the **Find all files** radio button, and select **Created**, **Accessed**, or **Modified** from the corresponding drop-down list box.

7. Click once on the **Between xx and xx** radio button to instruct **Find** to search the range of dates that you specify.

8. You might also want to click once on the **During the previous xx month(s)** radio button to instruct Find to search backwards over the number of months that you will specify.

9. You can also click once on the **During the previous xx days** radio button to instruct Find to search backwards over the number of days that you can also specify.

10. To narrow your search even further by searching by the file's size and type, click once on the **Advanced** tab.

> **NOTE**
>
> Entering information about the file's size is a quick way to limit a search. For example, if you are looking for a graphic file, you could select the **At least** selection from the **Size is** drop-down list and enter **3** in the **KB** spinner box (because most graphic files exceed this size). This will speed the search, because the computer will not bother itself with the hundreds of files that are smaller than 3 kilobytes (KB) in size.

11. Click once on the [Find Now] button to instruct Windows 98 to look for the file in question. Locations of matches

are placed in the box that appears immediately below the Find screen.

> **TIP**
>
> If you want to terminate a search before it is complete, just click once on the [Stop] button to do so.

Find Files on the Internet

1. Connect to the Internet via either the Windows 98 Dial-Up Networking feature to your local Internet service provider (ISP) or an online service such as AOL, MSN, or Prodigy.

> **NOTE**
>
> If you do not have any type of Internet connection, this search is not for you.

2. Click once on the [Start] button, and then select the **Find** menu selection. You will see the **Find** menu, which contains the various **Find** options.

3. Click once on the item labeled **On the Internet** to start the default Internet Web browser (probably Internet Explorer). Because you connected to the Internet in step 1, your Web browser automatically connects to Microsoft's World Wide Web site, which contains various Internet search engine options.

> **TIP**
>
> Notice that the search engine at the top of the list, which appears on the left side of the page, varies each time you exit the browser and then re-enter it. This is because Microsoft appears to be treating each search engine product on the list in an equal manner.

4. Click once on the engine that you want to use (for the sake of example, try **Infoseek**) and then type the search text in the box on the right side of the screen. Click once on the **Seek** button to start the search.

> **TIP**
>
> In case your search engine finds too many Web sites that match your search criteria, you can narrow your search. In the case of Infoseek, simply click the **Search Tips** hyperlink. Depending on which search engine you use, this hyperlink might have a different name to view information about making your search more effective.

5. After you get a search to return a manageable number of matches (you need to decide what is manageable to you; I find 10-12 pages an acceptable number to examine), click once on the **Search only within these *xx* pages** radio button (where *xx* equates to the number of pages returned as valid).

6. Scroll down the resulting screen to determine whether your search has been successful. When you reach the bottom of the screen, click once on the **Next 10** hyperlink to view the next 10 matches (assuming, of course, that there were more than 10 to begin with).

7. When you find a Web site that looks promising, you can view it by clicking once on its hyperlink.

Find a Computer on Your Network

1. Click the [Start] button, and then choose **Find**. You will see the **Find** menu, which contains the various **Find** options.

2. Click once on the second item, **Computer**, to open the Find: Computer screen.

3. Type the name of the computer you are looking for in the **Named** field and then click the [Find Now] button to initiate the search. When the Windows 98 search engine finds the computer that matches the search criteria, it places its name and location, as well as any comments about the computer (for Windows-based machines only), in the **found** box at the bottom of the search screen.

> **NOTE**
>
> Don't worry if you cannot remember the entire name of the computer you are seeking. Windows 98 is forgiving in this area. For example, suppose that you are looking for a computer named **Phaedrus** but, because you are unsure of the spelling, you simply type **Pha**. The Find Computer option will still come up with the correct answer.

Find People Locally

1. Click the [Start] button, and then choose **Find**. You will see the Find menu, which contains the various Find options.

2. Click once on the third item, **People**, to open the Find People screen.

3. You can perform your lookup via a person's name, email address, address (street address, city, state, and zip code are all rolled-up into one tiny data entry field), telephone number, or other text-based search criteria (to be defined by you). Enter your search criteria into any or all of these fields (obviously, the more information you enter, the narrower your search becomes), and then click once on the [Find Now] button to initiate the search.

> **NOTE**
>
> Notice that the [Web Site...] button is grayed out. This means that it is not usable in this portion of a "people" search. Keep in mind that you are searching within your own Personal Address book. This means that if you are not a big user of the Outlook Express email package that is built into Windows 98, then there are probably not going to be all that many names present in it.

Find People Globally

1. Click the [Start] button, and then choose **Find**. You will see the **Find** menu, which contains the various **Find** options.

2. Click once on the third item, **People**, to open the Find People screen.

3. Click on the drop-down list box next to the **Look In:** label to reveal the numerous Internet search engines. Select the one that makes you happy (all of them are quite good and quite bad all at the same time, so pick the one that sounds best to you).

> **NOTE**
>
> As soon as you select a search engine, you will notice a second tab appears down below in the search criteria area that permits **Advanced** searches. Also, take note that you can now only perform a basic search using a person's name and/or email address. All the other options have since disappeared as well.
>
> You can use the **Advanced** tab to further narrow an Internet-based search. Remember that each Internet search engine might contain fraudulent or otherwise misleading and incorrect data. So, do not take everything you find as being the truth.

4. Click once on the **Advanced** tab.

Change Internet directory service.

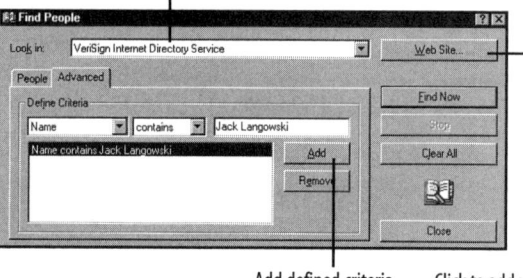

Add defined criteria.   Click to add your connect information.

5. A new screen appears containing the "hits" (data that matches your search criteria) from that particular search engine's database. To narrow this search more, type in the name of your target before retrying the search.

6. To find persons with common names, you might have to try many variations of the same search, so do not be discouraged if you are not completely successful the first time out.

> **NOTE**
>
> These search engines are only as good as their information (garbage in, garbage out). For the most part, they contain accurate and updated information, but not always.

FOLDERS

In the parlance of Windows 98, directories and subdirectories are known as *folders*. Simply put, folders are where all files and other directories are stored within Windows 98.

Explore Folders

1. To find the folder structure on your PC, right-click the **My Computer** icon and choose **Explore**.

> **NOTE**
>
> You use Windows Explorer to maneuver around your hard drive. Explorer enables you to move, copy, create, and delete files and folders as necessary. For more information about Explorer, see the section titled "Windows Explorer."

2. The My Computer window of Windows Explorer opens. Click once on the C: drive entry in the left column and the pane on the right will change accordingly. All the icons you see in this view are your folders.

FONTS

Fonts are used within Windows 98 to control how letters, numbers, and special characters look on the screen as well as when they are printed.

Install Fonts

1. Click once on the **Start** button, choose **Settings**, and then select **Control Panel**.

2. Double-click the **Fonts** icon in the Control Panel window to reveal that window.

3. Listed here are all the screen and print fonts that are already installed on your system. To add a new font to your system, click once on the **File** menu option, and then click once on the **Install New Font** menu selection.
4. The **Add Fonts** windows will then appear. In the bottom half of the window, find the folder or drive where the new font is to be installed.
5. In the **List of fonts** box, click any font that you want to install (click the [Select All] button if you want them all).
6. Check the **Copy fonts to Fonts folder** check box to create a copy of all the fonts that you are installing and to put that copy into the C:\Windows\Fonts folder.
7. Click the [OK] button to proceed with the installation.

Delete Fonts

1. Click once on the [Start] button, choose **Settings**, and then choose **Control Panel**.
2. Double-click the **Fonts** icon in the Control Panel window to reveal that window.
3. The **Fonts** window opens. Listed here are all the screen and print fonts that are already installed on your system. Right-click the font you want to delete, and then choose the **Delete** option from the shortcut menu. This will remove that font from your computer system.

FRONTPAGE EXPRESS

FrontPage Express is a tool for creating Web pages. Based on the full-blown Microsoft FrontPage 98 Web development tool, FrontPage Express makes it easy for first-time Web authors to create Web pages without having to learn the HTML programming language. For established Web authors, FrontPage Express is a great way to edit and enhance existing HTML documents.

Run FrontPage Express

1. Click once on the ![Start] button, choose **Programs**, **Internet Explorer**, and then **FrontPage Express**. This starts the FrontPage Express Web development tool.

2. If you are an HTML programming wizard, you can just start typing and create yourself a Web site. However, you will probably find it easier to modify an existing Web site to get the hang of things. To open a Web site, click once on **File**, and then select **Open**.

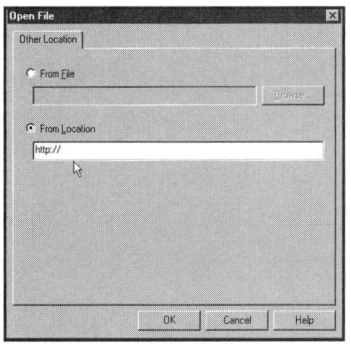

> **NOTE**
>
> Remember that all the text and graphical contents of companies' and people's Web sites are their own and copyright and trademark laws do apply. Therefore, although it is suggested that you use other Web sites for learning purposes, it is strongly recommend that you never ever use anyone else's work on your own Web site. The only time that it is even slightly acceptable to borrow from other Web sites is if you have obtained that Web site's written permission to do so. Failure to do this is, well, a bad idea at best.

3. The Open File dialog appears on your computer's monitor. If you want to find an existing Web page or site on your local computer or network, select the **From File** radio button. Then enter the pathname to the file in the corresponding text box (click **Browse** if you don't know the pathname).

4. Select the **From Location** radio button if you want to pull a copy of a Web page from the Internet or from an intranet/extranet. However, if this is your decision, you must manually type in the exact URL of the site you want to access (for example, http://www.microsoft.com/msdn).

5. After you enter that URL and click once on the [OK] button, retrieve the home page for whatever URL you choose directly into the FrontPage Express tool.

6. To examine the HTML code that makes the graphical features of the site possible, click once on the **View** menu option and then select the **HTML** menu selection.

7. The View or Edit HTML window appears. Examine the contents of this window to get a feel for how HTML operates.

> **NOTE**
>
> HTML code is neither as difficult nor as complex as it looks; it uses simple tags to format text and other elements of a Web page. For example, to place a title on your Web page, you will use the "**<title></title>**" format. To use this format, simply add in whatever text you want to appear in your title between these two < > markings. All the first **<title>** piece means is that you want to start your title here. The second **</title>** means that you have completed your title and want to end it. That is all there is to basic HTML. Take a closer look at various Web pages for ideas on how to format your own Web pages.

> **NOTE**
>
> If your goal is to quickly and easily create your own Web sites, it is strongly urged that you purchase a book on HTML as well as upgrade to the full Microsoft FrontPage 98 software package. This package provides many of the very advanced features found in Web sites around the Internet. For beginners, I would strongly suggest the book *Instant HTML* by Steve Wright (WROX Press LTD., 1996). For the more technical user, there is David Cohn's and Justin Higgin's book *Web Designer's Guide to FrontPage97*, which is excellent, even though it is one version old (Hayden Books, 1997).

8. To get a feel for a few of the features that you can pick up quickly, try clicking once on a graphical image to select it and then right-click on that same item to get a small menu to appear. Click once on the **Properties** menu selection to reveal the **Image Properties** screen.
9. This screen can be used to quickly change a graphical image that presently appears on this Web site, as well as to play with the quality of this same picture.
10. To save your changes and exit this screen, click once on the [OK] button.
11. Save your work by clicking once on the **File** menu option and then by clicking once more on the **Save As** menu selection.
12. This screen permits you to save your work directly back to the Web site that you grabbed it from, assuming that you have the proper permissions. Additionally, you can save this Web site to another location, which will then automatically activate the **Windows Publishing Wizard**.
13. Your final choice on this screen is to save your work under a completely new name somewhere locally on your hard disk drive.
14. After you have finished with your selections, click once on the [OK] button to save your page's title, location, and return to the main FrontPage Express screen.
15. Examine is the Page Properties screen, which can be accessed via the **File** menu option and then by a single click on the **Page Properties** menu selection. Doing this will take you directly into the Page Properties screen.
16. This screen permits you to alter the base location and default target frame for this Web page, as well as to set a background sound (and a few sound options) for this page.
17. After you have made your selections, click once on the **Custom** tab found on this same screen. Performing these steps causes the Custom screen to appear.

18. This screen is used to set the system and user variables for this Web page.

> **NOTE**
> A system variable is usually something that transcends the entire Web site, whereas the user variable is used to set basic descriptors and keywords for this particular Web site.

19. After you have finished with your review or making changes, click once on the OK button to save your alterations and exit this screen.
20. After you finish working on your Web page, either save it or discard it as an interesting learning experience.

GAMES

Windows 98 comes with four built-in games:

- FreeCell
- Hearts
- Minesweeper
- Solitaire

Any additional games you install on your PC might not be placed in the same folder structure as FreeCell, Hearts, Minesweeper, and Solitaire. Many games install into their own default locations, including games by Microsoft Corporation. However, for your own housekeeping purposes, you might want to install all your games into a subfolder of \Games to make finding them that much easier. Keep in mind, though, that not all of the games that you may install on your computer will give you the option of putting them someplace else on your PC, other than where that particular game manufacturer wanted to install them.

Play Games

1. Click once on the **Start** button, and then choose **Programs**, **Accessories**, and **Games**. Once there, you need to choose whichever game you want to play.
2. The game that you select will open on the Windows 98 Desktop. To start a new game, click the **Game** menu option and choose **New Game**.
3. If you need help learning how to play the game, click the **Help** menu option.

> **NOTE**
> As an alternative, you can press the F2 key on your keyboard to begin a new game.

> **NOTE**
>
> Starting any of Windows 98's other built-in games is much the same as starting FreeCell, except that when you want to start a new game of Solitaire, you select the **Deal** option in the **Game** menu.

GAME CONTROLLERS

In Windows 98, *game controllers* are devices such as joysticks, stick and rudder control systems, steering wheels, and the like.

Configure Game Controllers

1. Click once on the [Start] button, and then choose **Settings**, **Control Panel**.
2. The Windows 98 Control Panel window will appear. Double-click the **Game Controllers** icon to open that window. If you have no game controllers connected to your computer, the Game Controllers dialog will be empty.
3. If you are adding a game controller for the first time, you can use the **Add New Hardware** feature (refer to that section for more information). Otherwise, you can click once on the [Add...] button of the **Game Controllers** screen, which will take you to the Add Game Controller screen.
4. Click once on the option for the game controller that you are connecting to your PC and then click on the [OK] button, which will install the controller chosen. If your game controller is not listed, click on the [Add Other...] button to access the next screen.
5. Select the hardware you want to install or use the [Have Disk...] button to install the necessary device drivers from the floppy disk(s) or CD-ROM disc that came with your game controller. Click once on the [Next >] button to continue the installation process.

6. The Game Controllers dialog will display the hardware you have added. Click once on the `Properties` button to test each of the buttons, levers, and movement functions of your game controller.
7. To make port or controller changes to your game controller configuration, you will need to click once on the **Advanced** tab to access that screen's contents. The most important thing to keep in mind here is that if you do not understand the change that you are making, do not make the change. It is always better to consult the technical support information that came with the game controller or call the device manufacturer's help desk for further details.

> **NOTE**
> Most of the settings on this screen were probably established when you installed your game controller device for the first time. This is especially true if your device came with its own installation software, such as the Microsoft SideWinder Precision Pro joystick.

HARDWARE REQUIREMENTS

The hardware requirements for a Windows 98 computer are listed as follows:

- A computer that already has a DOS file allocation table created and has been formatted. This requirement is satisfied if your PC already has another version of Windows installed on it—such as Windows 95 or Windows 3.x—or if you are able to get to a DOS command prompt—such as c:\.
- An Intel or Intel-compatible 486DX-66MHz or faster microprocessor CPU.
- A hard disk drive that has at least 110MB of free space.
- 16MB of memory (commonly referred to as *RAM* or *DRAM*).
- VGA or higher-resolution monitor (preferably a color one).
- A high-density, 3 1/2-inch floppy disk drive.
- A CD-ROM disc drive if you plan to install Windows 98 from its CD packaging instead of from an endless series of floppy disks (using the Windows CD-ROM is the easiest method, and should be used if at all possible).
- A Microsoft mouse or compatible pointing device.

> **NOTE**
>
> If you are installing Windows 98 over an existing version of Windows, you are really performing an *upgrade* installation and not a new install. This might be important when you consider Microsoft typically charges less for upgrade versions of its operating systems than for full-blown new versions.

See Also Installing Windows 98

HELP

Windows 98 contains numerous interactive help screens, demos, quick hints, pop-up messages, and links.

Access Windows 98 Help

1. Click on the [Start] button and then select the **Help** menu selection.
2. Click on the **Contents** tab to view Help information in a table-of-contents—type format.
3. Click on any of the little books in the left pane of the window to view information that is more detailed regarding the high-level topics listed.
4. Click the **Index** tab to quickly jump to the topic for which you want more information.
5. Click to highlight an indexed item, and then click on the [Display] button to view information about the topic you selected.
6. Click the **Search** tab to search for help by entering a keyword. You would use this method when you are not sure what topic to look in for help.

HYPERTERMINAL

HyperTerminal enables you to connect to another computer system via a telephone line. In addition, HyperTerminal provides you with a fully functioning terminal window that can be used for controlling remote systems without any additional software. HyperTerminal also enables you to easily transfer files between you and another computer user, even if that other user has an old DOS-based PC.

Start HyperTerminal

1. Click once on the [Start] button, select **Programs**, **Accessories**, **Communications**, and then finally click once on the **HyperTerminal** menu selection to start the HyperTerminal application.

> **NOTE**
>
> Icons representing three HyperTerminal contact points will already be present in the folder: AT&T Mail, MCI Mail, and CompuServe. The fourth icon, HYPERTRM.EXE, represents the application you use to create new points of access. Double-click the **HYPERTRM.EXE** icon to continue.

2. The HyperTerminal *splash screen* shows itself and then disappears after only a few seconds. The splash screen is then replaced by the Connect To window. It is here that you will enter the information for the computer you are attempting to contact.

> **NOTE**
>
> *Splash screen* is a slang term for an entry screen—usually a pretty picture—to an application program.

Establish a HyperTerminal Connection

1. Click once on the [OK] button when you are certain that the information you have provided is correct.

> **NOTE**
>
> For your convenience, information in the Country code, Area code, and Connect Using sections of the Connect To dialog is pulled from information you provided when you enabled Windows 98 Dial-Up Networking features. You can alter any of this information simply by typing over the existing information.

2. Accept the default dialing properties or alter them as needed in the Connect screen (review the section entitled "Dial-Up Networking" for further details).

3. Click once on the [Dial] button to initiate the connection. The Connect message box will track the status of the connection. After the connection is made, you will be brought to the main HyperTerminal screen, which is where all contact with the remote system is made.

> **NOTE**
>
> Upon connection to the remote system, you can perform a variety of tasks including transferring files, chatting online, and controlling remote terminal connectivity. For more information about these topics, refer to a good telecommunications manual.

4. Press the ⏎Enter key once or twice (depending on who you are connecting to) to initiate the screen information and to know that you have connected. After you do this, the screen should begin to display information about your connection.
5. Enter a user ID and password identification to access a remote system, when prompted.

> **NOTE**
>
> When you have been established as a valid user, some systems will then prompt you for specific information regarding the features that your PC can handle (such as the number of lines per screen, characters per line that your PC screen is capable of showing, and whether your system can handle ANSI support). After this type of screen configuration is complete, you might be prompted for more detailed personal information or you might be taken directly into the practical aspects of the system to which you are connecting.

Disconnect a HyperTerminal Connection

Click once on the [Disconnect] button. Although the telephone connection has been terminated, it looks like nothing has happened.

Exit HyperTerminal

1. Click the **File** menu option and then choose the **Exit** menu. This will cause a message box to appear that prompts you to save your connection configuration.

2. Fill in a name for your connection to save it to your hard disk. You will be returned back to the HyperTerminal window from where you started, only now you will be able to see a new icon that represents your newly created connection.

> **NOTE**
>
> You may purchase the full version of HyperTerminal from Hilgraeve, Inc. (the makers of the slimmed-down version of HyperTerminal that comes with Windows 98). You will then have added functionality inside your version of the HyperTerminal application that does not exist in the form of the one that is built into the Windows 98 operating system. Visit them online at www.hilgraeve.com.

Connect to a Saved HyperTerminal Connection

1. Click once on the **Start** button, select **Programs**, **Accessories**, **Communications**, and then finally click once on the **HyperTerminal** menu selection to start the **HyperTerminal** application.
2. Double-click one of the HyperTerminal connection files (these files are the ones with .ht extensions) to use any of these HyperTerminal connections.

See Also Dial-Up Networking

INFRARED PROPERTIES

The infrared component of Windows 98 enables wireless communication between your PC and another computer. The catch here is that your computer must have a physical infrared port or device that can be configured for this type of communication. To install the infrared device, review the section titled "Add New Hardware Wizard."

Configure an Infrared Device

1. Click once on the [Start] button, and then choose **Settings**, **Control Panel**. The Control Panel window opens.

2. Double-click on the **Infrared** icon to access the first screen of the **Infrared Monitor** at the **Status** tab.

3. Click the [OK] button if you immediately receive a message indicating that there are no compatible infrared devices within range of your computer at this time.

> **NOTE**
>
> The term *within range* can mean different things to different computers. In general, the standard infrared range is 3–6 feet. Infrared ports should not have any obstructions, including window/clear dividers, between them.

4. Click the **Options** tab to view the set defaults for a generic Windows 98 infrared device. The second line, **Providing application support on COM5 and LPT3**, appears so that you can easily tell from where your infrared device will be "listening" for other infrared devices (for example, serial and/or parallel ports are where printers are found).

5. Click the **Preferences** tab to reveal the options available on that screen that, among other things, permit you to display an **Infrared Monitor** icon on the Windows 98 taskbar. You can then double-click on that icon to quickly return to the **Infrared Monitor** configuration screen.

6. Click the **Identification** tab to view a screen that enables you to change your computer's name and provide a brief description of it.

> **NOTE**
> Both infrared devices that are attempting to communicate with each other must have unique computer names. If a `duplicate name found` error occurs, you should change your computer's name in the **Identification** tab of the **Infrared Monitor** dialog.

> **NOTE**
> The computer description area is just an informational field that other users with infrared devices can scan to make sure that they are connecting to the correct computing device.

7. Click the `OK` button to make Windows 98 accept any changes that you made to the infrared configuration and return you to the desktop. If you checked the **Display the Infrared Monitor icon on the taskbar** check box in the **Preferences** tab, you will now see that **Infrared Monitor** icon on your Windows 98 taskbar.

INSTALLING WINDOWS 98

Windows 98 is very easy to install. The full version of Windows 98 will install from a CD-ROM onto a formatted hard disk with no operating system installed, although you can have DOS or some previous version of Windows (version 3.1 or newer) already installed. If your computer system is new and the hard drive is not yet formatted, consult the manuals that came with your computer for information on creating the system partitions and formatting the hard disk drive.

After you have completed the install, the first time you enter a User ID and a Password into Windows 98, you are creating these fields. In addition, if you do not use a password now, you will not be prompted for a User ID to logon in the future. Do not worry about typing in a password and then forgetting it. If you do not remember your password (or do not care to type one in), just press the (Esc) key and you will automatically bypass this whole logon process (so much for system security).

If your PC has a network card, the logon window will contain a third line that prompts you for a server or domain name. (If you do not know the server/domain name, contact your network administrator for further assistance). This password is important, because it is the one that will permit you access to your organization's network computing resources.

> **NOTE**
> All terminate-and-stay-resident (TSR) programs such as virus scanners and protectors, calendars, address books, and the like must be exited before you start the Windows 98 installation process. Consult the help manuals for each program for assistance in stopping these extra services. Additional information can be obtained from the Windows 98 Setup.Txt file that comes on the Windows 98 CD.

Pre-Installation Verification

1. Make sure that your computer meets the minimum hardware requirements for the Windows 98 operating system. This means that you must have at least 120MB of free hard drive space and 16MB of RAM (memory) on a PC with an Intel (or compatible) CPU. Your computer's CPU must be equal to an Intel 80486-DX processor that runs at least 66MHz.

2. Make sure that your computer has the minimum drive space available (somewhere from 165-225MB). Depending upon your installation method (that is, whether you are upgrading from Windows 95 or Windows 3.x; if this is a new installation with a FAT16 file system; or if it is a new installation with the FAT32 file system), you will probably require more drive space.

3. Confirm the existence of at least a disk operating system such as Microsoft DOS (the Windows GUI such as Windows 95 is preferred, because it will make the install process that much easier).
4. Prepare a formatted, blank, high-density, 3 1/2-inch, 1.44MB floppy disk to use for the creation of the Startup Disk during the install process.

Upgrade from Windows 95

1. Start your PC and let it start up completely into the Windows 95 operating system.
2. Place the Windows 98 CD in your CD-ROM drive. If you have autorun set on your computer, you can skip steps 3 through 5.
3. Click once on the [Start] button, and then choose the **Run** menu selection to open the **Run** pop-up box.
4. Type the command: `x:\Setup`, where *x* equals the disk drive letter of the CD-ROM disc drive.
5. Click once on the [OK] button to begin the installation process. This will start the Windows 98 Setup Wizard. (The Windows 98 Setup Wizard usually takes 30–60 minutes to complete, and might require you to restart your computer several times. Do not worry, this is normal for the Windows 98 Setup program.)
6. Follow all the prompts precisely as they are given on the screen, paying strict attention to the section on the creation of the **Startup Disk**.

> **NOTE**
>
> Although the Startup Disk might seem to be inconsequential to many, you will need this in case Windows 98 fails to start up at some point in the future. (Say, for instance, you accidentally delete some of the critical files on your computer such as Command.com.) Without the Startup Disk, you would not be able to get back into your computer, short of re-running the Windows 98 Setup program (not a good thing).

7. After the installation is complete and the system has been restarted, you will be presented with a **Welcome to Windows** logon screen. Enter your name and a password and then click once on the OK button to enter the Windows 98 operating system.

Upgrade from Windows 3.1x

1. Start your PC and let it start up completely into the DOS operating system.
2. Open the Windows 3.1x graphical user interface (GUI) application (for example, type **Win** at the C:\ prompt) if it doesn't proceed automatically.
3. Choose **Options, Run** to open the **Run** pop-up box.
4. Type the command: **x:\Setup**, where *x* equals the disk drive letter of the CD-ROM disc drive.
5. Click once on the OK button to begin the installation process. This will start the Windows 98 Setup Wizard. (The Windows 98 Setup Wizard usually takes 30–60 minutes to complete, and might require you to restart your computer several times. Do not worry, this is normal for the Windows 98 Setup program.)
6. Follow all the prompts precisely as they are given on the screen, paying strict attention to the section on the creation of the **Startup Disk**.

> **NOTE**
> Although the Startup Disk might seem to be inconsequential to many, you will need this system in case Windows 98 fails to start up at some point in the future. (Say, for instance, you accidentally delete some of the critical files on your computer such as Command.com.) Without the Startup Disk, you would not be able to get back into your computer, short of re-running the Windows 98 Setup program (not a good thing).

7. After the installation is complete and the system has been restarted, you will be presented with a **Welcome to Windows** logon screen. Enter your name and a password and then click once on the OK button to enter the Windows 98 operating system.

Upgrade from DOS

1. Start your PC and let it start up completely into the DOS operating system.
2. Insert the Windows 98 CD into the CD-ROM drive.
3. Choose **Options, Run** to open the **Run** pop-up box.
4. Type the command: `x:\Setup`, where *x* equals the disk drive letter of the CD-ROM disc drive.
5. Click once on the [OK] button to begin the installation process. This will start the Windows 98 Setup Wizard. The Windows 98 Setup Wizard usually takes 30–60 minutes to complete, and might require you to restart your computer several times. Do not worry—this is normal.

> **NOTE**
> Any applications on your computer might need to be reinstalled after the Windows 98 operating system is installed. In addition, it is possible that a few of your applications will not run at all under Windows 98. For a partial listing of applications that have trouble in the Windows 98 environment, review the Programs.Txt file on the Windows 98 Installation disc(s).

6. You are prompted for various default information, such as the name of the installation directory. It is strongly recommended that you leave the default choice of C:\Windows as the directory selection.
7. After the installation is complete and the system has restarted itself at least once, you will be presented with a Welcome to Windows logon screen. Enter your name and password, then click once on the [OK] button to enter the Windows 98 operating system.

See Also Help

INTERNET EXPLORER

Internet Explorer is the integrated Web browser that Windows 98 showcases.

Start Internet Explorer

1. Double-click the **Internet Explorer** icon located on the Windows 98 Desktop.

> **NOTE**
> If you have not yet connected to the Internet—either through a Dial-Up Networking client or through a direct connection, Internet Explorer will start the Internet Connection Wizard automatically; otherwise you will receive the Navigation Canceled error message in the title bar. If you have already connected to the Internet, you will see a screen that is populated with graphical information from Microsoft.

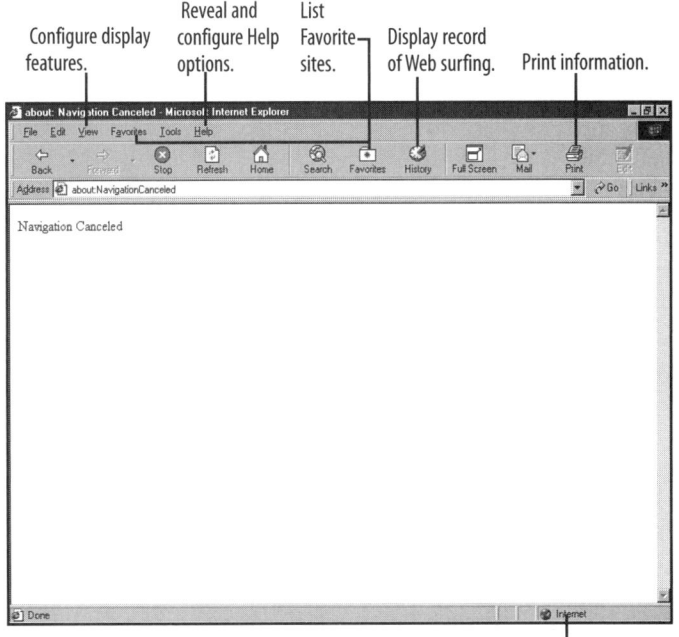

Reveal local Internet Security Zone setting.

2. Type a URL into the **Address** list box. For example, `http://www.mcp.com/` opens Macmillan Computer Publishing's Internet Web site. You can search for books that are dedicated solely to the topic of "Internet Explorer."

See Also Dial-Up Networking, HyperTerminal

ISDN CONFIGURATION WIZARD

ISDN stands for Integrated Services Digital Network, and is a special digital telephone line whose bandwidth can be much larger than that of the fastest analog modem. Typical bandwidths are 128Kbps (which translates to 131,072bps), as opposed to the fastest analog modem of 56Kbps (or roughly 57,600 bits per second). Quite a few of the smaller non-metropolitan areas (that is, those population centers with fewer than 50,000 people) in the United States do not yet support ISDN, so check with your local telephone company first before going out and spending a couple hundred bucks on an ISDN modem.

I don't know of any computer manufacturers that ship ISDN modems with their PCs. However, if you do happen to own an ISDN modem, use the Windows 98 ISDN Configuration Wizard application to configure it properly for use with the Windows 98 operating system environment.

You can use the Windows 98 ISDN Configuration Wizard to configure an ISDN modem for use with Windows 98. This wizard cannot be run until the hardware is installed in your computer, so make sure that this has been done before starting the wizard (refer to the section titled "Add New Hardware Wizard" for more information).

If you run this wizard and your modem still does not operate properly, you should consult the technical manuals that came with the ISDN hardware. Additional assistance can be obtained through your local telephone company or the manufacturer of the ISDN hardware.

Use the ISDN Configuration Wizard

1. Click once on the [Start] button.
2. Select **Programs, Accessories, Communications**, and then finally the **ISDN Configuration Wizard** menu selection.

> **NOTE**
>
> If you start the ISDN Configuration Wizard but do not have an ISDN modem, you will receive an error message telling you just that. If an ISDN modem is installed the wizard might work somewhat well, depending upon whether your proprietary ISDN modem works with the Windows 98 software (take a hint…most do not).

3. Follow all the prompts closely to complete the configuration of your ISDN modem.

See Also Dial-Up Networking, HyperTerminal

JAVA

Java is one of the latest computer languages for the Internet (originally developed by Sun Microsystems, Inc.), which allows small programs to execute on one's computer through an Internet Web browser (such as Microsoft Internet Explorer). Java generates extremely small executables (Java applets) to facilitate faster loading over potentially slow communications lines. Java contains built-in support for the Web, freeing the programmer from the burden of coming up with ad hoc solutions to common Web problems. Java is machine-independent and object-oriented and its syntax allows the programmer to generate modular, maintainable programs.

Java is not meant to be a full-blown development language such as Visual Basic or COBOL, but instead is more of a scripting language such as VB Script. Its use permits small to moderately complex Java applets to perform specific functions on an end user's browser, such as running a stock ticker.

See Also Internet Explorer, Java Console

JAVA CONSOLE

The Java Console menu option that is available from within the Microsoft Internet Explorer feature of Windows 98 is not a Java development editor. Rather, its purpose is to give the Web browser user a chance to see some basic information regarding the Microsoft Virtual Machine (VM) for Java (for example, this is where unhandled exception messages appear), which is built into Windows 98.

To access the Java Console, you first must open a Microsoft Internet Explorer window. To do this, click once on the **View** menu option and then click once on the **Java Console** menu selection. The Java Console window appears.

There is not much you can really do from the present implementation of Java Console except view some basic information regarding system priorities, threads, and memory usage. For example, if the letter **t** is typed first, it will automatically display the **Thread List** information (the lines that begin with "Pri").

Or, if the letter **m** is typed, the next two lines will display with the total and free system memory statistics.

Typing in the first letter of any of the options will cause that option to execute. For further details on any of these options, use the question mark (?) selection to start the Help option.

See Also Internet Explorer, Java

KEYBOARD

The keyboard that came with your PC, whether it is one of the older 82-key varieties or the latest ergonomically designed 101+ key masterpieces, is an important piece of hardware. Although it might appear to be working just fine, Windows 98 provides a few configuration options that can help you tweak your keyboard to make it a bit more to your liking. To configure your keyboard, do the following.

Configure Your Keyboard

1. Click on the **Start** button, then on the Settings menu option, followed by a single click on the Control Panel.

2. The **Control Panel** window will then appear. Double-click the **Keyboard** icon to access the first tab, the **Speed** tab, of the **Keyboard Properties** screen. Configure the **Character repeat** and **Cursor blink rate** settings to your liking on this screen.

> **NOTE**
>
> The **Character repeat** section of the **Speed** tab enables you to specify how quickly or slowly a character will repeat itself on your computer's monitor if you hold down that character's key. Use the test box on the screen to try out different settings to determine which setting is best suited to your tastes.

3. The **Cursor blink rate** area will enable you to specify how quickly or slowly the mouse cursor shown on your computer monitor blinks on-and-off. Play around with this setting until you discover the right one for you.

4. Click once on the **Language** tab to view that screen. Here you are able to specify what language you want to use on your PC (the default setting is **English (United States)**.

> **NOTE**
>
> You can specify that any of a number of languages be used, and you can increase the number of available languages by installing Windows 98's five additional language-support features (Baltic, Central European, Cyrillic, Greek, and Turkish). For information about installing these features, use the Windows Setup portion of the **Add/Remove Programs** feature to add these additional language options (once there you will need to access the Multilanguage Support option).

5. To add another language, click once on the `Add...` button and follow the prompts.

> **NOTE**
>
> If you install a language that you do not understand, it is possible to completely mess up your computing environment. This can be fixed only through this **Keyboard Properties** screen. So, either memorize where the various buttons you will need to use on that screen are placed, or make sure that you are fluent in the language you are installing.

6. After you are satisfied with your settings, click once on the `OK` button to exit the Keyboard Properties dialog.

> **NOTE**
>
> On the latest and greatest keyboards that ship with standard PC systems these days, come a variety of additional, special keys, which can be used to perform a wide array of activities. These activities include things as diverse as setting the volume on your speakers, to printing screens of information, to quickly accessing the Windows 9x **Properties** menu option, and the list goes on. Some of these keyboards will use the standard Windows 98 Keyboard Properties screen to modify their settings, while others (such as the one you can find on the Hewlett-Packard Kayak Workstation) require the use of proprietary software in order for you to enable/disable/alter the settings of certain keyboard functions.

See Also Add/Remove Programs

KODAK IMAGING

The imaging component of Windows 98 has a variety of uses:

- It acts as the software for scanning information into your PC.
- It enables you to view, print, and manipulate received faxes.
- It enables you to view and print several types of graphical images.

> **NOTE**
> Eastman Software Company, a division of Kodak, Inc., wrote the imaging software that Microsoft licensed and integrated into its Windows 98 product.

Use Imaging Software

1. Click once on the **Start** button, select **Programs**, **Accessories**, and finally select **Imaging**. The main **Imaging** window will appear. It is from this main screen that all of your viewing, editing, and/or printing of graphical images will be done.
2. To view or print a graphical image that you already have on your computer, choose **File, Open**.
3. Next, you should navigate to the Windows 98 folder that contains the image you want to view or print.
4. Click once on the **Open** button to open the file that you have selected, and voila! The image will appear inside the **Imaging** window.
5. Print the image by selecting **File, Print**.

Contact Kodak

1. Click once on **Help** and then again on **About Imaging** to access that screen's contents.
2. Click once on the **Contact Info** button to obtain the necessary information.

LINKLOCAL NETWORK IP ADDRESS

If you happen to work in a small business or other organization where multiple personal computers are in use, you might want to consider building a small network based on the Internet protocol known as TCP/IP. The reason for doing this is that you will be better able to share information between yourself and your colleagues with minimal configuration (beyond that of actually installing the hardware, which could be as simple as an Ethernet network card in each PC, connected to a centralized hub).

You can assign automatic private IP addresses for a simple network via the Windows 98, using Microsoft's latest TCP/IP networking technology known as the LINKLOCAL network IP address space. This technology assigns a unique IP address to your network interface card (NIC) with a TCP/IP format of 169.254.x.x (where each *x* equates to one octet of the full IP address; the first half of the IP address will always be formatted as 169.254).

These LINKLOCAL network IP addresses can be used only on privately maintained internal local area networks (LAN) and can never be used on the Internet. To configure your Windows 98 PC to use this technology, review the section on "Network Protocols" in this book. Essentially, what you will be doing is configuring your Windows 98 PC to dynamically assign or accept a TCP/IP address from a DHCP server.

> **NOTE**
> A LAN without at least one server is considered a peer-to-peer network, which means that all logon and access security must be controlled on each individual PC.

See Also Network Protocols, TCP/IP

LOG OFF WINDOWS 98

The logoff process for Windows 98 is useful only when multiple persons use the same computer. If only a single user works on a certain PC, the shut down process would be used instead.

In the event that multiple persons use your PC, you should log off by doing the following.

Log Off Windows 98

1. To log off a Windows 98 PC, click once on the [Start] button and then click **Log Off <User Name>** (where **<User Name>** equates to the logon ID of the person who is attempting to log off).

> **NOTE**
> The current user's name automatically appears, so you do not need to figure out who is already logged on to the computer.

2. You will see a confirmation screen. Click once on the **Yes** button to confirm that you want to log off this Windows session.
3. Windows 98 will shut down all the active programs and return you to the standard Windows 98 login screen. It is here that the next user can log onto this Windows 98 PC.

See Also Log Onto Windows 98

LOG ONTO WINDOWS 98

To log onto a Windows 98 PC, just start your PC. When Windows 98 starts up, this process is the same as logging on if this is a home computer. If you are connected to a network of some sort, you will be prompted to actually log onto a specific computer network, such as Windows NT or Novell NetWare (you will see a login screen that prompts you to enter a User ID, Password, and perhaps even a default server name).

See Also Log Off Windows 98

MAIL CONFIGURATION

Electronic mail (email) is the method by which you can communicate in writing with another user anywhere on the planet. This communication can occur via a corporate network or via the Internet.

Configure Email

1. Right-click on the **Internet Explorer** icon found on the Windows 98 desktop and choose **Properties** from the shortcut menu that appears.

2. Click once on the **Programs** tab of the **Internet Properties** screen to reveal the contents of that window.

> **NOTE**
>
> The **Messaging** area enables you to choose which email package you want to use with the Internet Explorer browser, as well as which Internet news and call software you want to use.

3. Click once on the down-arrow button to the right of the **Mail** text box to view the drop-down list box, which lists the available email software packages that are compatible with the IE browser.

4. Click the email package of your choice to select it and then click once on the OK button to accept the changes, which will then close the **Internet Properties** window.

See Also Outlook Express Email Client

MAINTENANCE WIZARD

The Maintenance Wizard utility enables you to schedule the use of some of the more time-intensive maintenance utilities such as the Disk Defragmenter, ScanDisk, the Compression Agent, and so forth. The nice thing about this wizard is that it contains several of the more powerful

Windows 98 disk performance-enhancing applications including:

- Compression Agent (for use only with DriveSpace3 Drives)
- Delete Unnecessary Files
- Disk CleanUp
- Disk Defragmenter
- ScanDisk

If, by chance, you have already installed the **Microsoft Plus! 98** add-on software for Windows 98, an additional component will appear inside your version of the **Maintenance Wizard**:

- Clean Up Your Start Menu (this includes finding broken links)

You can schedule these tools individually, without the use of the Maintenance Wizard utility, but use of the wizard will definitely make the configuration process easier.

> **NOTE**
> The Maintenance Wizard tool is not included in a default Windows 98 installation. The three default categories are Speed Up Programs, Check Hard Disk for Errors, and Delete Unnecessary Files.

Use the Maintenance Wizard

1. Access the Maintenance Wizard utility by clicking on the Start button, then the **Accessories menu** selection, then **System Tools**, and then on the **Maintenance Wizard** menu selection. After you click on the Maintenance Wizard menu selection, its initial setup screen will appear.

2. After the Maintenance Wizard window appears, either click once on the top radio button, **Perform Maintenance Now**, to begin the maintenance configuration immediately, or click once on the bottom radio button to change the schedule option. The default setting is to perform the maintenance now. Then, click once on the `OK` button to start the process.

3. If you selected the **Perform Maintenance Now** radio button in the previous step, the Maintenance Wizard started processing the various tasks. Alternatively, if you chose the **Schedule** radio button, you will see the Express/Custom Configuration screen. At this screen in the wizard process, you can either select the **Express** setup configuration (this is the default) or the **Custom** option. I recommend you click once on the **Custom – Select each maintenance setting myself** radio button.

4. After you have made your selection, click once on the `Next >` button to continue.

> **NOTE**
> If you had chosen the **Express** setup configuration option, the Maintenance Wizard would have skimmed through all of these steps automatically, leaving you with little or no input as to how your PC would be configured. For the extreme beginner this might be okay, but for the rest of the world, it is always good to know what is going on with your computer.

5. Choose a time to run these disk maintenance tasks, or, if you have used this screen at least once previously, you may keep your current timing schedule by clicking once on the **Custom – Use current settings** radio button option. Make your selection, and then click once on the `Next >` button to continue.

> **NOTE**
>
> If you have purchased and installed the Microsoft Windows 98 Plus! Add-on software package onto your Windows 98 PC, you will see an additional screen. Otherwise, this screen will not appear as an op-tion for you. The purpose of this screen, the **Start Menu Cleanup** utility, is to remove any dead links (or shortcuts) that might exist in your menus, as well as on your Windows 98 Desktop. This is a useful utility, one that might even justify the $49 cost of the Microsoft Windows 98 Plus! application. Make your selections and any changes to the scheduling of this tool by using either the [Reschedule...] or the [Settings...] button, and then click once on the [Next>] button to continue the configuration process. If you do not see this screen, do not worry, as it is not part of the standard Windows 98 operating system.

6. The Speed Up Programs dialog will now appear. This is where you define the settings for the Disk Defragmenter application. Make your selections and any changes to the scheduling of this tool by using either the [Reschedule...] or the [Settings...] button. Click once on the [Next>] button to move on.

7. The ScanDisk utility appears. This is where one defines the settings for the ScanDisk application (refer to the ScanDisk section of this book if you do not understand what it can do for you). Make the selections and any changes to the scheduling of this tool by using either the [Reschedule...] or the [Settings...] button, and then click once on the [Next>] button to continue the configuration process.

8. The Delete Unnecessary Files window shows up. This section permits one to define the settings for the Disk CleanUp application. Make your selections and any changes to the scheduling of this tool by using either the [Reschedule...] or the [Settings...] button, and then click once on the [Next>] button to continue the configuration process.

9. The final screen of the Maintenance Wizard appears. This is where you review your settings, and then end the wizard. If you place a check mark in the box at the

bottom of this screen, all the scheduled tasks will be run for the first time as soon as you click on the [Finish] button. Click once on the [Finish] button to complete the Maintenance Wizard process. The Maintenance Wizard utility will close completely if you did not tell it to run your scheduled tasks. Otherwise, it will begin executing all the scheduled tasks in order. This process could easily take several hours to complete, so do not start it if you are planning on working hard at your computer for the next few hours.

See Also Disk CleanUp, Disk Defragmenter, ScanDisk

MAKE COMPATIBLE

There is a little known tool built into the Windows 98 operating system known as the Make Compatible utility. This tool does exactly what you might think it would: it makes older Windows 3.1 applications work and print properly under Windows 98. It is quite amazing that this tool gets little or no press at all from Microsoft, given its capabilities.

The Make Compatible utility can help you make that old screen capture utility work fine under Windows 98 or let you use that older 16-bit version of QuickBooks with Windows 98 (because now it will print correctly). Keep in mind, however, that you should not be using this tool to try to get old, non-compliant application development debugging tools as well as disk utilities to work with Windows 98. The side effects of doing such a thing can be devastating not only to your application, but also perhaps even to your entire Windows 98 computer system.

Use Make Compatible

1. Maneuver your way to the \Windows\System folder on your hard drive and look for the Mkcompat.exe file.

2. After you find the **Make Compatible** utility, double-click on it to execute it. This will take you into the main screen for this tool.

3. Select an executable (*.exe or *.com) file to make it compatible with this tool.

> **NOTE**
>
> In step 3 you must determine the name of the file that runs your particular application. For example, say you were trying to use Collage Capture 1.0, which was made by Inner Media, Inc. in 1993, with Windows 98. Although it is an excellent screen capture program, its compatibility out-of-the-box with Windows 98 is questionable at best.

4. To find the executable program you want to make compatible with Windows 98, click on **File**, and then **Choose Program**. This takes you into the Choose Program window.

5. Maneuver your way through your Windows 98 PC folders until you find the program you need. This part might be a guessing game, especially if you have never developed software (and thus have no feel for figuring out which program does what for a specific application). After you have located the file you want to use (which will probably end in either the .exe or .com formats), click once on that file to first select it and then click once on the [Open] button to pull that file into the Make Compatible program.

6. Choose one of these options:

    - **Lie About Printer Device Mode Size**—This is great for those applications that blow up whenever you try to print from within them.

    - **Lie About Window's Version Number**—This is an overall nicety, which fools older programs into thinking that they are still running in a Windows 3.x environment.

    - **Win 3.1 Style Controls**—Not every program out there can handle the Minimize, Restore, and Close options found in the upper-right corner of every Windows 95/Windows 98 screen.

7. To select any of these options, click once on the box next to the option you want so that a check mark appears in that box.

8. After you have everything you want, click once on the **File** menu option, followed by a click on the **Save** menu selection.

9. To locate all the additional settings that the Make Compatible application has available, choose **File, Advanced Options**. This causes the advanced features to be displayed.

10. Several of these are great for older applications, especially the old DOS programs that you may have developed yourself years ago in FoxPro 2.0, Turbo Pascal, or Visual Basic for DOS. The more popular selections include:

    - **Enable 3.x UI Features**—Pretty obvious as to what this one does.
    - **Disable EMF Spooling**—This is a printer feature.
    - **Increase Stack Size**—This should get you around those invalid stack size error messages that you see a lot with old DOS programs.
    - **Windows 3.1 Palette Behavior**—This aids in color resolution problems that you might encounter with some graphics packages.

11. Click once on **File, Save** to save your work. Otherwise, you should just close this utility.

12. If you have not yet saved your work, you will be prompted to do so by the **Make Compatible** message box.

13. If you want to save your work, click once on the [Yes] button, otherwise choose the [No] button.

MICROSOFT NETWORK

Microsoft Network (MSN), a business unit of Microsoft Corporation, is one of the online services (AOL, AT&T

WorldNet Service, CompuServe, and Prodigy Internet are the others) that is available for installation as part of the Windows 98 operating system. When Windows 98 is loaded, pointers to these five services are installed to ensure the availability of the software for these services. However, unlike the other four online services that are available, The Microsoft Network can be more readily installed, because its initial icon exists directly on the main Windows 98 Desktop.

Install and Sign Up for Microsoft Network

1. Double-click on the **Setup MSN** icon that appears on your Windows 98 Desktop. This will start the **Microsoft Network** installation process. A small informational box might appear asking you to insert your Windows 98 CD-ROM disc into your CD-ROM disc drive.

> **NOTE**
> The MSN software requires a few files from that CD to install the required software. It might take a few seconds before the Microsoft Network software starts to install onto your computer, so try to be patient.

2. The first screen you see (Windows 98 Desktop) will have a dark background and will contain several prompts instructing you to follow the rest of the Microsoft Network installation process. Use these online instructions to complete the configuration and signup process. Keep in mind that the Microsoft Network online service is not a free one, and that you will be required to input information from one of your credit cards to actually signup for MSN.

3. Upon completion, you will probably be required to restart your PC. Do so to complete the installation process.

See Also America Online (AOL), AT&T WorldNet, CompuServe, Prodigy Internet

MICROSOFT PLUS! 98

Just like Windows 95, there is a Plus! Package for the Windows 98 operating system. Its name: Microsoft Plus! 98 (very original). This is where the similarity between the Windows 95 and Windows 98 versions ends. The Microsoft Plus! 98 package, when fully installed, will consume 188.8 megabytes of hard disk drive space (it can only be purchased in a CD-ROM format, whereas the old Windows 95 Plus! Package came on just six floppy disks). Heck, the Microsoft Plus! 98 software programs, when fully loaded, actually take up more space than all the original Windows 95 operating system including the six disks worth of the Microsoft Plus! 95 add-on tools and games.

Microsoft Plus! 98 comes with a whole lot of neat utilities, games, screen savers, and even an antivirus package. The components are as follows:

- Compressed Folders (just like WinZip)
- Deluxe CD Player (much better than the standard Windows 98 version)
- Desktop Themes (95MB worth of graphics, noise, and interesting screen savers)
- Disk CleanUp Add-Ons (a few extra features for the Windows 98 Disk CleanUp feature)
- Golf 1998 Lite (a scaled-down version of Microsoft Golf)
- Lose Your Marbles (definitely a new favorite Windows game)
- Maintenance Wizard (a few extra features for the Windows 98 Maintenance Wizard feature)
- Organic Art Screen Saver (just like it sounds!)
- Picture It! Express (a scaled-down version of this good graphics tool)
- Spider Solitaire (another addictive Windows solitaire game)
- Virus Scan (the McAfee Antivirus software package, which comes with six months worth of free updates)

MODEM PROPERTIES

The term *modem* literally means *modulator-demodulator*. In plain English, a modem is a hardware device that translates the bits of information from your computer into bits of data that an analog telephone line (such as the one you call your mom on every week) can understand enough to transport it to another computer's modem (where the process is reversed).

To see what modems you have installed in your computer and for a quick lesson in determining whether a modem is working, follow the steps listed next.

Use Modems Properties

1. Click once on the **Start** button, and then choose **Settings, Control Panel**.
2. When the Windows 98 Control Panel window appears, double-click on the **Modems** icon, to reveal the Modems Properties screen.
3. To determine whether a specific modem is properly communicating with Windows 98, click once on the **Diagnostics** tab.

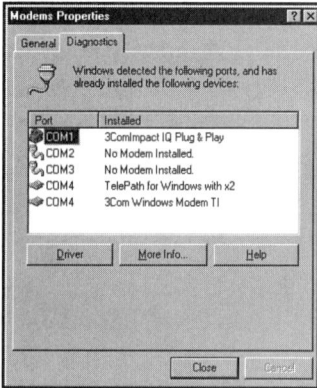

> **NOTE**
>
> If the top box in the **General** tab of the Modems Properties dialog is empty, that means no dial-up modems are properly installed in your computer. However, it is possible to have a cable modem installed and working properly, but not appearing in the box (although this is not the norm).

4. Select a modem by clicking on its port, and then click the ◉ button to check the communications capabilities of that modem.

5. The More Info screen will appear. If the modem is working properly, this screen will contain useful information. For instance, you can determine which communications port and interrupt request your modem uses. Otherwise, you will see nothing in the box. Click once on the [OK] button to return to the previous screen.

> **NOTE**
>
> If no responses are indicated in the box at the bottom, it is likely that the connection between your PC and the modem has failed or that your modem is not working properly. (This can be because the wrong software drivers are loaded or because the modem is broken.)

6. Click once on the **General** tab in the Modems Properties dialog, and then click the [Properties] button to review and configure the highlighted modem in the *Modem Name* Properties dialog. The General tab enables you to set the maximum speed at which the modem should attempt to connect and how loud your modem is when it connects.

> **NOTE**
>
> If you have a 19.2Kbps modem, setting it at 57.6Kbps will not make your modem work faster; it will only tell Windows 98 that maybe your modem can transmit information faster than it actually can. This can result in errors during the transmission process, which can actually result in your modem processing data at a lower bandwidth than it is normally capable of doing!

7. Click once on the **Connection** tab to view information about how the parity data bits are set, how your call preferences are set, how the port settings are configured, and how the advanced settings are configured.

> **NOTE**
>
> Windows 98 does an excellent job of configuring the settings in the **Connection** tab whenever a new modem is installed, so if you do not understand these complex terms, you can safely leave them alone.

8. Click once on the **Distinctive Ring** tab to access that screen, which enables you to configure how the modem will sound if you are using it for inbound telephone calls. If you do not see this tab on your screen, it simply means that your modem does not support this feature.

> **NOTE**
>
> In order for you to be able to configure your modem sounds, your telephone line must support distinctive ring services. Check with your local telephone company for more information. If no **Distinctive Ring** tab appears on your *Modem Name* Properties dialog, it indicates that your modem device is incapable of supporting this option.

9. Click once on the **Forwarding** tab to view that screen's contents. If applicable, click once on the **This phone line has Call Forwarding** check box and then type in the proper activation and deactivation codes for your line (your local telephone company should provide these codes to you).

> **NOTE**
>
> In order for you to be able to enter information in the **Forwarding** tab, your telephone line must support call forwarding. Check with your local telephone company for more information. If no **Forwarding** tab appears on your *Modem Name* Properties dialog, it indicates that your modem device is incapable of supporting this option.

10. Click once on the [OK] button to accept your changes. You are then returned to the **General** tab of the Modems Properties dialog.

11. Click once on the [Dialing Properties] button to open that screen, which is where you may set the location(s) from which you are dialing. Also, you may configure any special codes that must first be dialed to reach an outside line, to disable call waiting or caller ID, or to use a calling card.

12. After you are satisfied with your selections, click once on the [OK] button to return to the Modems Properties dialog, and then click once on this final [OK] button to accept your changes.

MOUSE PROPERTIES

The mouse is one of the most important pieces of hardware on your computer system. Without one, it is virtually impossible to be productive on a Windows 98 PC. Most mice have two buttons: a primary one (usually the left button) and a secondary one (usually the right button). Obviously, if you are left-handed, you will want the primary button to be your right button and the secondary to be on the left. Some mice have a third button or a rolling ball or wheel (as is the case with the Microsoft IntelliPoint mouse) in the middle.

To configure your mouse to best suit your needs, install it according to your mouse manufacturer's specifications. More than likely, your mouse has a tiny attachment on the end of the mouse cable that will only plug into one port on the back of your PC. If by chance, your mouse's connection looks just like the one for the keyboard, refer to the documentation that came with the computer to figure out which spot the keyboard plugs into (the one that is left over is where you plug in your mouse). Next, install the software drivers that came with the mouse that you purchased (if this is a new computer with pre-installed software, chances are that your mouse software has already been installed for you as well). To actually use the Windows 98 features for configuring the your mouse, follow this next set of steps.

Configure Your Mouse

1. Click once on the [Start] button, and then choose **Settings, Control Panel**.
2. When the Windows 98 Control Panel window appears, double-click on the **Mouse** icon, to reveal the Mouse Properties screen.

> **NOTE**
>
> The example in the next several steps assumes you have a Microsoft IntelliPoint mouse, which has a rolling wheel in addition to primary and secondary buttons. If you do not have this type of mouse, many of these steps (screens) will vary. In those cases, consult the documentation that came with your mouse so that you can configure it for Windows 98.

3. The **StepSavers** tab of the Mouse Properties dialog is probably the first thing you will notice, which has four timesaving options: **SnapTo, Focus, ClickSaver,** and **SmartSpeed**. These features give you the ability to make things happen faster, with fewer mouse clicks or movements. Carefully read each option before making your choices.
4. Click once on the **Pointers** tab, which enables you to change how your mouse pointer appears onscreen. To change your mouse pointer, click the down-arrow button next to the **Scheme** text box to view a drop-down list of available pointer schemes.
5. Click once on the [Apply] button to accept the scheme that you have selected.
6. Click once on the **Basics** tab, which is where you can specify how quickly your pointer moves, the primary and the secondary (this is useful if you are left handed), and the double-click speed.
7. Click once on the **Visibility** tab, which is used to specify whether you want your pointer to vanish while you

type, to display pointer trails, or to automatically wrap to the opposite edge of the screen when you start a new line.

> **NOTE**
>
> In step 7, you can also select the Sonar option, which displays a target around your mouse pointer whenever you press the Ctrl key once on your keyboard. (This can be helpful on those busy or colorful screens, such as you might find inside video games.)

8. Click once on the **Productivity** tab to access those options.

> **TIP**
>
> A personal favorite of mine is the Odometer section, which lets you see how far your mouse pointer has traveled across your monitor since the day you installed it. It does not really enhance your productivity, and some might say that it detracts from it, but I still like it.

9. Click once on the **Wheel** tab to access those options. To change the button features of the wheel, click once on the down-arrow button to the right of the **Button Assignment** text box, and then select from the drop-down list of tasks the wheel can perform:
    - Double-click
    - Get help (F1)
    - Start Windows Explorer
    - Open the **Start** menu

    Press the wheel once and the action you assigned should occur instantly.

10. Click once on the Apply button to accept changes to the mouse wheel.
11. Click once on the OK button to exit the Mouse Properties screen.

See Also Accessibility Options

MULTI-LANGUAGE SUPPORT

Microsoft Windows 98 provides a series of options that permit the support of languages other than English within the operating system. To install the language options, use the **Windows Setup** tab of the Windows 98 Add/Remove Programs utility to add them (if you do not know how to do this, refer to the "Add/Remove Programs" section found in section A of this book).

MULTIMEDIA PROPERTIES

The multimedia features of Windows 98 allows a computer to handle audio and video content in a pleasing manner, as well as to provide you with a more user-friendly way in which to learn new things and perform new tasks.

To view multimedia content in Windows 98, you can use the Windows Media Player that comes with the operating system. However, you would be wise to use the Windows Update feature of Windows 98 to obtain the latest version of this utility; it permits the playing of a multitude of multimedia types.

See Also Windows Update

MY COMPUTER

The My Computer icon found on the Windows 98 Desktop provides you with a quick means of exploring your computer. Double-clicking on this icon will bring up an Explorer-type window that will then allow you to peruse your hard drive just as you can with the normal Windows Explorer utility. When you open it, you can quickly see lots of information about your computer system such as how big your hard drives are, how many drives you have, any network drive mappings you might have, and so on.

See Also Network Neighborhood

NET WATCHER

Net Watcher enables you to monitor other computer users who are accessing resources on your network. Moreover, Net Watcher permits you to see those resources, such as folders, that are "shared" (that is, made available to the rest of the network). This feature applies only to users who are connected to a network, so if you do not have a network connection, this feature is not for you.

Before running the Net Watcher utility, you must have Client for Microsoft Networks installed with the **File** and **Print Sharing** options enabled.

Run Net Watcher

To run Net Watcher, do the following:

1. Click once on the [Start] button. Choose **Programs, Accessories, System Tools**, and **Net Watcher**. The main Net Watcher screen appears.
2. To select the computer to monitor, choose **Administer, Select Server** to open the Select Server window.
3. Type in the name of the computer that you want to administer. If you do not know the name of the computer you wish to administer, click once on the [Browse...] button to view the Browse for Computer screen.
4. Navigate to the computer you want to administer, and then click once to select it.
5. Click once on the [OK] button to return to the Select Server window; the server you selected now appears in the **Name** text box.
6. Click on the [OK] button again to confirm your selection.
7. You will then return to the main Net Watcher screen. Clicking the toolbar buttons along the top of the screen will present you with different views of the shared resources, and will show you who is accessing those resources at any given time. If you click once on the [icon] button, you will be able to determine which folders are shared with those who connect to your computer.

> **NOTE**
>
> The 🔍 button looks like a small manila folder with someone's outstretched hand holding it, along with a tiny magnifying glass peering into the same folder. If you place the tip of your mouse pointer on top of this button and just wait a second, the ScreenTip "Show Shared Folders" will automatically appear (so you will know that you are about to select the correct button).

> **NOTE**
>
> The button directly to the right of the 🔍 button is known as the 📋 button. This option is a quick way to view those files that someone has opened on your system, which folders those files were shared from, as well as who presently is accessing them. To access this feature, click once on the 📋 button.

See Also Network Neighborhood, Resource Meter

NETMEETING

Windows 98 comes with a handy communication tool called NetMeeting. This program allows you to participate in those ever-popular chat sessions similar to Microsoft's Comic Chat; but NetMeeting takes communicating online to a whole new level. It allows you to participate in private conference calls and true working meetings with people anywhere using the Internet or your company's intranet/extranet.

In addition to the standard typing chat session, NetMeeting lets you use your PC like a telephone using your PC's microphone and speakers. In addition, with the right video equipment, you can even see each other. NetMeeting also incorporates powerful tools to help your collaborate on projects by sharing documents and applications, transferring files back and forth, and through use of a whiteboard that is visible to all of the parties in your call. All this without having to pay expensive long-distance telephone charges.

In this section, you learn how to set up and use the NetMeeting feature, which is installed automatically on your PC during a *full* installation of Windows 98. If you didn't do a full installation, you need to install NetMeeting using the Add/Remove Program. If you need information on how to do this, review that section in this book.

To help you get up and running, NetMeeting comes with a handy Configuration Wizard. Just closely follow the wizard and the steps here, and you will soon be well on your way to communicating with others across your organization, over the Internet, and around the world.

> **NOTE**
> Before you get started, you should confirm that your computer hardware is compatible with NetMeeting, especially in the video camera, microphone, and other audio equipment areas. Compare your computer's hardware with Microsoft's listings of approved (meaning tested) hardware that you can find on their Internet Web site at: http://www.microsoft.com/netmeeting/.

Configure NetMeeting

1. Click once on the [Start] button. Select **Programs, Internet Explorer, NetMeeting** to start the initial Microsoft NetMeeting Configuration Wizard informational screen.
2. Click [Next >] to move to the Directory Server Entry screen.
3. Choose the **directory server** that you want to use. It is important that everyone you want to participate in the conference call uses the same host directory. Click [Next >] to move on to the next screen.

> **NOTE**
> It is the name of the computer that will be hosting the Internet conference-call meeting. It is suggested that you use the default server provided by Microsoft Corporation until you find or create others for your own purposes.

4. Enter the personal information here that you consider appropriate and that will identify you to the other participants on this server. To continue with the wizard process, click [Next>].

> **CAUTION**
>
> Before you get too excited about entering your personal information here, remember NetMeeting is only a *suggestion* that you use your real information. Don't forget that whatever you type here is going to be readily available to anyone on this server. You could always input Chicago Cubs as your first and last name and WorldSeries@1999 (always a great thought, I might add) as your email address, if you want. It is meaningless content, but so what!

5. Select a **Category** to describe the type of sessions you intend to use: **Business Use, Personal Use [Suitable for All Ages]**, or **For Adults-Only Use**. Click once on the [Next>] button to move to the next screen.

> **CAUTION**
>
> Be forewarned, the For Adults-Only Use category, as the name suggests, could contain a high pornographic or sexual content. If you want to protect your children from content that might be objectionable, you should choose **Personal Use [Suitable for All Ages]**.

6. Click the radio button for the speed that most closely represents your network or Internet/intranet connections. Either select **Local Area Network** (if you are connecting through your company's network) or select the type of modem that you have on your computer. Click [Next>] to move to the next screen.

> **TIP**
>
> If this is not accurate, you could lose data and you could find yourself bogged down in unwanted graphics.

7. Select your primary video capture device (or camera). Click [Next>] to move to the Audio Tuning Wizard.

> **NOTE**
> You must close all other applications that play or record sounds, such as the CD Player or Sound Recorder, before starting the Audio Tuning Wizard.

8. Position the **Volume** slider bar to adjust the speaker volume for your calls. Click once on the `Test` button, to test your setting. When you like what you hear, click `Stop` (formerly the `Test` button). Click `Next >` to move to the Record Volume screen.

9. Position the **Record Volume** slider bar, and begin reading the test sentence into the microphone. You should be able to use your normal speaking voice. Click `Next >`.

10. You will see an error message telling you what to do if there were problems adjusting your sound levels. Otherwise, you can simply click `Finish` to enter the main Microsoft NetMeeting screen.

Use NetMeeting

1. After you have established a connection to the Internet or to your network, you can open NetMeeting by clicking the `Start` button, and choosing **Programs, Microsoft NetMeeting**.

2. Immediately after entering the NetMeeting application, you should look at the right side of the status bar to determine whether you are logged on to one of the servers. If you don't see a **Not logged on**, click **Tools, Options** and click on the **Calling** tab. Select the server from the drop-down list. Be patient, it might take a little while to actually log on.

> **NOTE**
> NetMeeting should already contain the information you want from the wizard process. However, if you do decide to change any of your information, just click **Call, Change My Information**. All of the information you entered in the wizard can be found and edited here, with two exceptions.

3. To join a call in progress, double-click any of the directory entries with an asterisk (*) to the left side of the computer monitor icon. The (*) means that this person also connected.

> **NOTE**
> Of course, you can try to contact anyone, but don't be surprised if a lot of contact tries end up in failure because that person didn't respond to the call. In addition, the people in a call can reject your entry to that conference, so do not be surprised if you cannot find a call to join. Likewise, you can ignore or reject calls from other people that you don't wish to talk to.

4. If you would rather, you can always create your own call by clicking the [button] button and following the simple prompts.

> **TIP**
> If you get tired of strange people calling you constantly, you can elect to hide your email address from the directory listing, which anyone can readily access and view. People can still contact you, but they must already know your email address. Choose **Call**, **Change My Information**, and click on the **Calling** tab. After making the appropriate selections on this screen, click [OK] to return to the main NetMeeting screen.

5. At the New Call dialog, enter the email name, computer name, or network address of the person you want to call in the **Address** text box.
6. Select the method you want to use to place your call from the **Call using** drop-down list, and click [button].
7. If the person you are calling is logged on to the same server, your call will begin. If not, you will receive an error message. (Just click [OK] to get rid of that.)
8. After you get a call going, you can access the **Whiteboard**, **Chat**, and **Collaborate** features all from the toolbar. If at least one of the parties has the appropriate equipment, you can also hear and view them.

9. To complete your conference call, simply use the **Hang Up** icon on the toolbar.

See Also Add/Remove Programs

NETWORK

With the increasing use of Internets, intranets/extranets, LANs/WANs, and peer-to-peer networks, you might be wondering what all the fuss is about. Networking is basically a way to allow one computer to communicate with another. This can be an invaluable tool for sharing information and resources with a group of individuals, for example, over the Internet.

Before you can begin using networks, you will need to understand their components and to configure your computer to communicate properly with your server. Let's start with a bit of a glossary.

- **Network:** The network is that platform that links multiple computers via cables.
- **Adapters:** Adapters are the specific pieces of hardware (can be physical or virtual), such as Network interface cards (NICs) and cables, which actually connect your computer to the network.
- **Protocol:** The Protocol, such as NetBEUI or TCP/IP, is the "language" that one computer uses to communicate with another computer.
- **Clients:** A client is the software that your PC uses to interpret the information received from the server and to share files and printers. Different browsers and other Internet software use and require different client software.
- **Service:** Services enable you to share automated services and resources over a network.
- **Primary Network Logon:** This is the language, or client, that you will use to authorize your log on to the network.

Now that you understand the networking components a little bit better, let's look at your PC's network configuration.

Review Your Network Configuration

1. Access the Windows 98 Control Panel by clicking the [Start] button, and then **Settings, Control Panel**.
2. At the Control Panel screen, double-click the **Network** icon to reveal the Network Properties screen.

> **NOTE**
>
> Notice the message window titled, `The following network components are installed.` This shows your current network configuration. The listing contains (from top to bottom) all the networking client software (small computer icons), the various (NICs) or network adapters (small network card icons), and the networking protocols (small cable-looking icons).

3. Click on the [Add...] button to select a component to add to your PC. (We will talk more about this later.)
4. Click on a component and you can either click [Remove] to take the component out of your configuration or click [Properties] to view the settings for your components.

> **CAUTION**
>
> The settings shown in the Properties screens are very specific and fairly advanced. It would be wise not to play with these. If you need to change something, contact your ISP (Internet service provider) or your network administrator to walk you through. It is amazing how hard it can be to fix an error here.

5. To change your **Primary Network Logon**, select the appropriate logon from the drop-down list of available networks.
6. To turn file and printer sharing on or off, click the **File and Print Sharing** button. You will be asked to select whether you want to let others share your files and/or your printer. When you are finished, click [OK].

7. Click **OK** to change your new settings and close the dialog. Alternatively, click **Cancel** to exit without making changes.

See Also Network Adapters, Network Clients, Network Neighborhood, Network Protocols, Network Services

NETWORK ADAPTERS

A Network Adapter is a piece of hardware, such as Network interface cards (NICs) and cables, which actually connects your computer to the network. Luckily, Windows 98 provides a common interface method, the Network dialog, and hundreds of software drivers for installing network adapters to your computer.

> **TIP**
> Keep in mind that these network adapters can be real, physical cards that are physically installed inside your PC or they might be virtual cards. For example, they could be logical devices that are software-created and that exist only in your computer's memory systems.

Add a Network Adapter

1. Access the Windows 98 Control Panel by clicking the **Start** button, and then **Settings**, **Control Panel**.
2. At the Control Panel screen, double-click the **Network** icon to reveal the Network Properties screen.
3. Click on the **Add...** button, and double-click on **Adapters** (small network card icons) from the Select Network Component Type screen.
4. Notice that the Select Network Adapters screen is divided into a right and left pane. Select your Adapter from the **Manufacturers** list. (Note that the adapters currently on your PC are the first on the list.)

5. Select the **Network Adapters** from the right pane. If you have the required drivers on disk, click [Have Disk...]. If not, skip to step 7.
6. At the Install From Disk screen, you will be asked for the location of the driver. If you are not sure, you can click [Browse...] to search for your file. When finished, click [OK].
7. If the driver is already on your hard drive somewhere, you can simply click [OK] on the Select Network Adapters screen to return to the main Network dialog.
8. Notice that your adapter has now been added to the list of installed components.
9. Usually, you will need to restart you computer before the changes will take effect. Close any open applications, and then click [OK].

See Also Network, Network Neighborhood, Network Clients, Network Protocols, Network Services

NETWORK CLIENTS

A client is the software that your PC uses to interpret the information received from the server and to share files and printers. Different browsers and other Internet software use and require different client software. The Windows 98 operating system makes it easy to add and remove new client software, including both the built-in clients as well as third-party clients.

Add Network Client Software

1. Access the Windows 98 Control Panel by clicking the [Start] button, and then **Settings**, **Control Panel**.
2. At the Control Panel screen, double-click the **Network** icon to reveal the Network Properties screen.
3. Click on the [Add...] button, and double-click on **Clients** (small computer icons) in the Select Network Component Type screen.

4. Notice that the Select Network Client screen is divided into a right and a left pane. Select your **Client** from the **Manufacturers** list.

5. Select **Network Clients** from the right pane. If you have the required drivers on disk, click [Have Disk...]. If not, skip to step 7.

6. At the Install From Disk screen, you will be asked for the location of the driver. If you are not sure, you can click [Browse...] to search for your file. When finished, click [OK].

7. If the driver is already on your hard drive somewhere, you can simply click [OK] on the Select Network Clients screen to return to the main Network dialog.

8. Notice that your client software has now been added to the list of installed components.

9. Usually, you will need to restart you computer before the changes will take effect. Close any open applications, and click the [OK] button.

See Also Network, Network Neighborhood, Network Adapters, Network Protocols, Network Services

NETWORK NEIGHBORHOOD

The Windows 98 Network Neighborhood displays all the computers that are presently connected to your local and wide area networks. The Network Neighborhood makes it easier to share resources among the computers on the network.

Run Network Neighborhood

1. Double-click the **Network Neighborhood** icon on your Windows 98 Desktop to access the primary **Network Neighborhood** window.

2. This window displays an icon for each PC on the network, as well as one for the entire network. Click once on one of the **PC** icons to view a description of that computer along the left side of the window.

3. To close this window, click once on the × button in the upper-right corner of the window.

Map a Network Drive

1. Double-click the **Network Neighborhood** icon on your Windows 98 Desktop to access the primary **Network Neighborhood** window.

> **NOTE**
>
> To explore Network Neighborhood's other options, right-click the **Network Neighborhood** icon on the Desktop to view its shortcut menu. Among other things, this menu enables you to quickly map a network drive. When you map a drive, it means that a new "logical" drive letter is assigned to a direct path to the server-based resources.

2. Click once on the **Map Network Drive** option. This opens a screen where you need to type the name of the server and its shared resource in the following format:

    \\server name\resource name

> **TIP**
>
> A resource is a file, folder, or fax/printer that another computer is sharing with you.

3. Click once on the [OK] button to map the drive. That is all you need to do.

See Also Network, Network Neighborhood, Network Clients, Network Protocols, Network Services

NETWORK PROTOCOLS

The Network Protocol is the "language" that one computer uses to communicate with another computer. Windows 98 has an advantage over the Windows 95 operating system, in that it supports several additional packet transport protocols, which are simply known as **Network Protocols**.

Luckily, Windows 98 provides a common interface method for installing all its networking components, whether they are network adapters, network clients, network services, or networking protocols.

Add Network Protocols

1. Access the Windows 98 Control Panel by clicking the `Start` button, and then **Settings**, **Control Panel**.
2. At the Control Panel screen, double-click the **Network** icon to reveal the Network Properties screen.
3. Click on the `Add...` button, and double-click on **Protocols** (small cable-looking icons) in the Select Network Component Type screen.
4. Notice that the Select Network Protocol screen is divided into a right and a left pane. Select your **Protocol** from the **Manufacturers** list.
5. Select the **Network Protocols** from the right pane. If you have the required drivers on disk, click `Have Disk...`. If not, skip to step 7.
6. At the Install From Disk screen, you will be asked for the location of the driver. If you are not sure, you can click `Browse...` to search for your file. When finished, click `OK`.
7. If the driver is already on your hard drive somewhere, you can simply click `OK` on the Select Network Protocol screen to return to the main Network dialog.
8. Notice that your Network Protocol has now been added to the list of installed components.
9. Usually, you will need to restart you computer before the changes will take effect. Close any open applications, and click the `OK` button.

See Also Network, Network Adapters, Network Clients, Network Neighborhood, Network Services

NETWORK SERVICES

A network service enables you to share automated services and resources over a network. Windows 98 has an advantage over the Windows 95 operating. Luckily, Windows 98 provides a common interface method for installing all its networking components, whether they are network adapters, network clients, network services, or networking protocols.

Add Network Services

1. Access the Windows 98 Control Panel by clicking the `Start` button, and then **Settings**, **Control Panel**.

2. At the Control Panel screen, double-click the **Network** icon to reveal the Network Properties screen.

3. Click on the `Add...` button, and double-click on **Service** (small computer icons with bar in front of them) in the Select Network Component Type screen.

4. Notice that the Select Network Service screen is divided into a right and a left pane. Select your **Service** from the **Manufacturers** list.

5. Select the **Network Services** from the right pane. If you have the required drivers on disk, click `Have Disk...`. If not, skip to step 7.

6. At the Install From Disk screen, you will be asked for the location of the driver. If you are not sure, you can click `Browse...` to search for your file. When finished, click `OK`.

7. If the driver is already on your hard drive somewhere, you can simply click `OK` on the Select Network Service screen to return to the main Network dialog.

8. Notice that your Network Service has now been added to the list of installed components.

9. Usually, you will need to restart you computer before the changes will take effect. Close any open applications, and click the `OK` button.

See Also Network, Network Adapters, Network Clients, Network Neighborhood, Network Protocol

NOTEPAD

Notepad is a basic text editor. It lets you type and print text, but unlike a word processor, it does not have any formatting features available. It's streamlined small size does offer two advantages that the bigger word processors can't beat, however, it opens fast and it won't drain your resources even if you leave it open to make notes throughout the day.

Use Notepad

1. Click once on the **Start** button.
2. Select **Programs**, **Accessories**, **Notepad**.
3. To begin using the **Notepad** application, just start typing as soon as the program starts and you see the white screen background.
4. Create a new file by choosing **File**, **New**.
5. Open an existing file by choosing **File**, **Open**.
6. In the Open window that you will now see, navigate to the file you want to open, click it once to select it, and then click once on the **Open** button. The file you selected will now open inside the Notepad screen. Make changes to the text as needed.
7. To save the file, click once on **File** and then on **Save**.
8. To print the file, click once on **File** and choose **Print**.
9. To close the file, click once on **File** and choose **Close**.

See Also WordPad

ONLINE USER'S GUIDE

Windows 98 comes with an electronic version of its user manual. This electronic version of the user manual is known as the *Online User's Guide*. This guide covers many more topics, and in a much greater depth, than the cheesy user's guide that ships with the Windows 98 operating system. Additionally, the online version comes with a very good search capability that permits you to find the information that you require fast.

Access the Online User's Guide

1. Click once on the [Start] button and choose **Help** to reveal the primary Windows Help screen.

2. Click once on **Getting Started Book: Online Version** to reveal the **Microsoft Windows 98 Getting Started Book** hyperlink. Then double-click that hyperlink to view the book online.

3. After this book is open, you will be able to jump around among the topics quickly and without any difficulty. Simply double-click on the topic that interests you, and it opens automatically.

> **NOTE**
>
> There are three tabs at the top of the window: **Contents**, **Index**, and **Search**. Entry-level Windows 98 users will probably find the **Contents** tab most useful, because it contains little books on each general topic area (such as Using a Mouse, Internet Basics, and a Glossary). Intermediate users (former Windows 95 or Windows NT Workstation users) should enjoy the layout of the **Index** tab. This tab permits them to type the specific topic about which they need information, and it will appear in the list below. Advanced users of Windows 98 will find the **Search** tab the most useful. Here, they can obtain a listing of the topics that are available for a specific "higher-level" topic. Regardless of your user level, all the tabs are readily available to you.

See Also Windows Help

OPEN DATABASE CONNECTIVITY (ODBC)

Open Database Connectivity (ODBC) is a programming interface standard used for connecting computer applications to a database (such as Microsoft Access or Microsoft SQL Server) that supports the SQL language. The ODBC standard has been around for several years (almost an eternity in the computing world). It is a commonly accepted way to connect applications with databases as diverse as Oracle, Informix, Sybase SQL Server, Microsoft Access, and Microsoft SQL Server.

Configure ODBC

1. Click once on the **Start** button. Select **Settings**, and then **Control Panel** to reveal that screen.
2. Double-click on the **32-bit ODBC** icon in the Control Panel window to access the **ODBC Data Source Administrator**. This dialog contains the following tabs:
   - **User DSN**—This tab enables you to add, remove, or configure user data sources. User data sources store information about how you connect to the indicated data provider. Only you can view your user data sources, and they can be used only on your current machine.
   - **System DSN**—This tab enables you to add, remove, or configure system data sources. The system data sources work just like user data sources, except that they are visible to all users and services on the PC.
   - **File DSN**—This tab permits you to add, remove, or configure file data sources. A file data source enables you to connect to a specific data provider.

> **NOTE**
> Adding and deleting system data sources works much the same as adding and deleting other data sources.

- **ODBC Drivers**—This tab enables you to view the ODBC drivers installed on your system. This screen is for informational purposes only. To add or remove an ODBC driver, you must use the instructions that came with that driver's installation disk(s).
- **Tracing**—This tab enables you to set tracing parameters. An ODBC trace should be used whenever you suspect that a certain ODBC driver has a problem. Selecting the **All the time** radio button in the **When to trace** area is not recommended, because this will create extra overhead for the computer.
- **About**—This tab contains information about all the ODBC core components.

3. To add or remove a data source, click the appropriate tab on the ODBC Data Source Administrator screen.
4. Click once on the data source you want to add or remove to highlight it.
5. Then click once on the [Add..] or [Remove] button, depending on which action you want, and then carefully follow the prompts.
6. Click once on the [OK] button to accept your changes and to close the ODBC Data Source Administrator screen.

OUTLOOK EXPRESS ADDRESS BOOK

Windows 98 comes with a POP3 email package known as Outlook Express, which includes a nice little Address Book. You can store email addresses of your friends, acquaintances, and so on, along with detailed information about those contacts (such as full name, address, telephone and fax or pager numbers, as well as little notes that you may devise on-the-fly). Using the Microsoft Outlook Express Address Book is not at all difficult, because most of the content that you need to fill-in is based on common sense. Use these instructions and you will soon be an expert Outlook Express Address Book user.

> **NOTE**
> POP3 is an electronic message standard known more formerly as the "Post Office Protocol", version 3.0. Most of the 130+ commercial versions of UNIX support this Internet standard manner of messaging, as do many other computer vendors such as Novell or IBM. Various Microsoft products actually support a few different messaging standards such as POP3 and MAPI (Messaging Application Programming Interface).

Access the Address Book

1. Click once on the **Start** button, then on **Programs, Internet Explorer, Outlook Express**. Otherwise, you could also access the Outlook Express application by clicking once on the Outlook Express icon that appears on the Windows 98 Quick Launch toolbar.

2. Click once on the **Address Book** icon that appears along the top menu button bar. You might be prompted with a default vCard Viewer message box. If you use the full-blown Microsoft Outlook client application, you will be prompted to set it as the default.

> **CAUTION**
> It is recommended that you do not make this Address Book the default for your computer system, especially if you use your other messaging application for work or other specially developed applications. If you click once on the check box, you will no longer be prompted by this message box regardless of the answer that you give now.

3. To continue, click once on either the **Yes** or the **No** button (depending upon your choice, which means that if you select the **Yes** button Outlook Express will become your default email system), which will then take you directly into the main screen of the Outlook Express Address Book.

4. To view information about any of the names listed in your Address Book, click once on any of the names, which will then display a small box with that person's full name and email addresses.

5. To add someone new to the Address Book, click once on the 🗋 button (the one on the far-left side of the top menu bar), this will take you into the Properties screen for an **Address Book** contact.

6. The **Personal** tab is used to enter the basic personal data that can be saved along with someone's email address. Click once on the **Send E-mail using plain text only** box to select it. This option is necessary for those recipients who cannot receive email in any format except as a text basis (ASCII).

7. After you have made all your entries/changes, click once on the **Home** tab to continue. Here, you may save information regarding your contact's address, telephone numbers, personal Web page, and gender. After you have made the desired entries and/or changes, click once on the **Business** tab.

8. Here you are able to save information regarding your contact's business address, telephone numbers, business Web page, and job position. After you have made the desired entries and/or changes, click once on the **Other** tab to continue.

9. Use this screen to store notes regarding your Address Book contact. After you have made all the desired entries and/or changes, click once on the **NetMeeting** tab.

10. This screen permits you to define a default NetMeeting server as well as a listing of all other NetMeeting servers that are available for meeting-up with this contact. After you have made all you're desired entries and/or changes, click once on the **Digital IDs** tab to continue.

11. Select an email address to use with your Digital ID information.

12. Click once on the [Import...] button to add a digital ID for use with this account. After you have made all your entries and/or changes, click once on the [OK] button to complete the process and return to the main Address Book screen.

13. A quick way to send someone mail from your Outlook Express Address Book, is to click once on that person to select him/her, and then right-click once to reveal a small pop-up menu.
14. Next, click once on the **Send Mail** menu selection, which will then take you directly into a **New Message** screen where you will see this Address Book contact already inputted into the **To:** address box. Complete the text, add the attachment(s), if necessary, and then click once on the **Send** button and you are done!

See Also Email, Outlook Express Email Client

Import Contact Information

1. To start the import process, select **File, Import, Address Book**.
2. Select the origin of the Address Book data that you want to import by clicking on it once to highlight it.
3. Click once on the [Import...] button and the process will commence immediately.

> **NOTE**
> If you are attempting to import Address Book data from a Microsoft Exchange Server client (such as Microsoft Outlook 97 or 98), you might be prompted by a Choose Profile screen.
>
> If you are not importing from an Exchange Client software package, chances are you will see no notification of the progress of the import process. However, when the process is complete you will be notified by an Address Book Import message box.

4. As soon as the process finishes, click once on the [OK] button to acknowledge the end of the import process and close this message box. You will then see all your newly imported Address Book contacts inside the Outlook Express Address Book.

See Also NetMeeting

OUTLOOK EXPRESS EMAIL CLIENT

Configuring Microsoft Outlook Express for use with a POP3 email service provider, such as your Internet service provider (ISP), is not too difficult and takes only a few minutes of your time. You begin by accessing the Microsoft Outlook Express application, and then using the configuration screens to create a new "Account" for your ISP connection. After this is done, all you need to understand is how to quickly compose, send, receive, and read your email messages.

> **NOTE**
>
> POP3 is an electronic message standard known more formerly as the "Post Office Protocol", version 3.0. Most of the 130+ commercial versions of UNIX support this Internet standard manner of messaging, as do many other computer vendors such as Novell or IBM. Various Microsoft products actually support a few different messaging standards such as POP3 and MAPI (Messaging Application Programming Interface).

Configure Microsoft Outlook Express

1. Click once on the [Start] button, and select **Programs, Internet Explorer, Outlook Express**. This will take you into the first screen of the Microsoft Outlook Express configuration process.

2. Choose a folder in which to place your Outlook Express files. After you have made your selection by clicking on the destination folder, click once on the [OK] button to continue into the Microsoft Outlook Express application.

3. After the primary screen of Outlook Express opens, you can quickly figure out the basics just by looking at it. Over to the left is a tree-like structure that permits quick access to all the folders within the application: Inbox, Outbox, Sent Items, Deleted Items, and Drafts. (A draft is a message that you have composed and closed, but did not send yet.)

4. Moving on, you will want to select **Tools, Accounts** to access the Internet Accounts window. After it opens, click once on the **Mail** tab (the Internet Accounts windows should open with the Mail tab showing).
5. Click once on the [Add...] button to reveal a small menu, which contains three options: **Mail, News,** and **Directory Service** (all three of these menu selections are used to create new mail, news, and/or directory service accounts). Click once on the **Mail** menu selection to access the first screen of the **Internet Connection Wizard**.

> **NOTE**
> If you have already established an Internet email account, you will not automatically go straight into the Internet Connection Wizard.

6. On this first screen, you need to fill in a descriptive name for the new Internet email account that you are creating. You would usually put in the name of the ISP or the person that it is most used by/for. After you have entered a name, click once on the [Next >] button to continue the process. This will take you to the screen where you can enter your full Internet email information.
7. On this screen, you need to type the complete Internet email address that was assigned to you by your email administrator or Internet service provider (ISP). After you have entered this information, click once on the [Next >] button to continue the process.
8. At this point, you need to determine whether the Internet email account you are configuring is of the POP3 or IMAP type.

> **NOTE**
> POP3 is version 3.0 of the Post Office Protocol (an Internet standard), whereas IMAP is the Internet Mail Addressing Protocol. When in doubt, choose POP3 because the vast majority of Internet email accounts use this third version of the POP protocol.

9. Use the drop-down list box to make your incoming Internet mail server type selection. Then enter in the full name of your POP3 or IMAP incoming mail server in the top box, and the outgoing SMTP mail server's name in the lower box.

10. After you have entered the data required, click once on the [Next>] button to continue the process.

11. Typically, you need to enter your user ID and password into the top two boxes, which will then permit you to be authenticated by your ISP's Internet servers. However, should you be connecting to a non-POP3 email server, you will then need to click once on the bottom radio button. This will let you logon using the Secure Password Authentication (SPA), however, you will want to check with your ISP to confirm that SPA will work with your configuration.

12. Make your entries as necessary, and click once on the [Next>] button to continue the process.

13. A Friendly Name is simply a descriptive name that you use to describe your newly created Internet email account that appears within the Outlook Express Accounts list. After you have input the text that you want, click once on the [Next>] button to continue the process.

14. The **Internet Connection Wizard** continues by prompting you to select an **Internet Connection Type**. To choose one, click on the radio button next to the type that is required for you to connect your PC to the Internet. The top choice requires the use of a telephone, whereas the second means that you are using a network connection, and the third signifies that you do not wish to change a selection that you already have in place (that is, you will need to manually establish your own connection each time you want to use Outlook Express).

15. After you have made your selection, click once on the [Next>] button to continue the process.

16. Review the information on this screen and then click once on the [Finish] button to end the wizard.

17. To continue into the advanced configuration process, click once on the email account that you just established to select it. Next, click on the [Properties] button, which will take you to the screen.

18. The first screen is informational in nature. However, you should pay close attention to the check box located near the bottom of this screen. It is labeled **Include this account when doing a full Send and Receive**, which means that whenever you click on the [🗐] button or menu option, you will be trying to send all the messages associated with this email account as well as receiving all those messages that are addressed to this account.

19. After you have made your changes, if any, click once on the **Servers** tab to proceed with the wizard process. The purpose of the Servers screen is to review the various server entries that were made during the initial setup of the email account. Changes can be made to any of the server settings, as necessary, with only the new area of information being the possible use of additional authentication required for your outgoing mail server. To continue, click once on the **Connection** tab.

20. On the Connection tab, you are able to alter the default connection type for this specific email account. If you click once on the radio button next to the **Connect using my phone line** option, you are able to specify a default Dial-Up Networking connection in the drop-down list box.

21. Click once on the **Security** tab to access the email account security options screen.

22. The Security screen permits you to configure a digital signature for use with your Outlook Express email account. To create a digital signature, click on the top check box to select it, and then fill in the box located just below this section (it has the [Digital ID...] button to its left).

23. Next, click once on the **Advanced** tab to continue.
24. The top options on this screen permit you to change the port numbers of your incoming (POP3) or outgoing (SMTP) email servers. Typically, you will not need to change either of your port addresses, but if this does become necessary, it is nice to know where this setting is found. In addition, you are able to designate the use of SSL (Secure Sockets Layer) for either or both of these email servers. SSL is a level of encryption that provides for the secure transfer of email between your PC and the email server to which you are connecting. (Your server must already provide this capability. It is not a one-sided affair!)
25. Click once on the [OK] button to complete the advanced configuration process to take you to the main Microsoft Outlook Express screen. Well, almost, anyway. Chances are, that if this is the first time you have run Outlook Express or if you have another email package installed on your PC, you will encounter one final message box.
26. If you want Outlook Express to become your default messaging client software, click once on the [Yes] button. Otherwise, click once on the [No] button. In either case, click once on the check box to select it if you want Outlook Express to automatically check to see if it is still the default email package on your PC every time it is started. Make sure that you check (or uncheck) this box, *before* you click on either the **Yes** or **No** options. After you make your selection, you will then immediately be taken to the main Microsoft Outlook Express screen.
27. If you have previously installed other email software packages, Outlook Express will detect them and attempt to perform a conversion of that software's address book and/or existing messages. Of course, if it is an old or proprietary package, Outlook Express will not be able to make these conversions work. Also, if you do

not have any other packages installed (or ever had any installed), you will be taken directly into the main screen of the Microsoft Outlook Express email system. Otherwise, you will be presented with the first screen of the Outlook Express Import Wizard.

28. If you want to import both messages as well as addresses from your existing email system, just leave both of the check boxes marked (as is the default). Otherwise, click once on the option that you wish to unselect. After you have made your decisions, click once on the [Next >] button to continue.

29. On this next screen, use the drop-down list box to select the Microsoft Outlook profile to which you want to convert the messages and/or address book. After you have made your selection, click once on the [OK] button to continue the process.

30. You may make a selection to work online or offline, provided that you have a local mailbox. Otherwise, if your mailbox is stored only on your messaging server, you will need to select the Online mode. After you have made your decision, follow the few short prompts that will follow (it is all wizard-based). On completion, you will be taken directly into the main screen of the Microsoft Outlook Express package.

31. When opening the primary screen, you will see the Inbox for the Outlook Express package. Click on the **Inbox** once to select it, and you will notice two email messages. These are the two default messages that Microsoft automatically places inside everyone's Outlook Express email mailbox, which tout the security and messaging features of Outlook Express. If you double-click on one of these, such as the **Welcome! Message**, you will be able to review that message (which, by the way, is how you access any email message in your Outlook Express Inbox).

32. After you have read this message, close it just as you would close any Windows 98 message window. (Hint: Try the x in the upper-right corner of the window.) After you are back on the main Outlook Express window screen, click on the 🗔 button's drop-down list box down arrow.

33. A drop-down menu box appears where you are able to create a new message using the special stationery that comes with Outlook Express or no stationery at all. Click on the option you want (with stationery, you just select a type of stationery); it will then take you into a New Message window with that stationery shown in the background.

34. The first step in composing a new message is deciding to whom you want to send the message. Click once on the **To** area so that you are able to enter the recipient(s) name(s), which must be separated by a semicolon (if there is more than one recipient).

35. You can, of course, click once on the little index card icon located at the start of the **To** area, which will permit you to select recipient name(s) directly from the Outlook Express Address Book.

36. To select a recipient, click once on that person's name to select it, and then click once on the appropriate button (the **TO:**, **CC:**, or **BCC:** buttons). If you need more information regarding the use of the Address Book, you might want to review that section of this book.

37. After you have made all your selections, click once on the [OK] button. This will take you back to your new message, keeping the names of all the recipients that you selected.

38. From this point, all you need to do is type in a **Subject** (this is an optional field) and the message itself. Click once on the **Send** button (located near the top-left side of the **New Message** window).

> **NOTE**
>
> A neat feature of Outlook Express is that it can automatically detect what your default email message type is for the recipients that you have input into your **Address Book**. For example, if you have some Internet-based recipients who can only receive plain text (ASCII) messages, sending that type of person an HTML-based file would be worthless. Luckily, the Outlook Express application that comes with Windows 98 takes care of all this technical stuff behind-the-scenes automatically.

39. After you have sent a file, it will move to the Microsoft Outlook Express **Outbox**.

40. The number in the parentheses to the right of the label **Outbox** represents the total number of messages that exist in your **Outbox** awaiting transmission to their ultimate destinations. After those messages are transmitted (after the Send/Receive session completes), these messages will automatically disappear from the Outbox.

41. If you click once on the **Sent Items** icon in the Outlook Express tree (in the column on the left, just below the **Outbox** icon), you will be able to review the messages that you have recently sent.

42. All the items in this area have already been sent via your messaging server to their ultimate destinations. Underneath the column **Sent**, you will see the exact time and date that the message was transmitted from your PC and started its journey towards its destination.

43. If you highlight a message and then either press the `Del` key on your keyboard (it might be abbreviated as `Del`) or drag it over to the Deleted Items icon, that message will be removed from your system. Well, almost, anyway. You guessed it! That message now resides in the Deleted Items area of Outlook Express and will remain there until you empty your trash.

OUTLOOK EXPRESS MAINTENANCE TASKS

During the use of Outlook Express, you might want to know how to use the compacting tool; how to import email messages, address books, and/or other mail account settings; how to export email messages and address books; or configure the Inbox Assistant. These are a few of the maintenance items that should be attended to once you start using the Outlook Express messaging application. Failure to perform these maintenance items will not necessarily result in the crash of your Windows 98 PC, even after months or years of neglect, but they might cause your computer to operate a bit more sluggishly than it otherwise would have. All these maintenance items can be started from within the main Outlook Express screen, using the general toolbar that is at the top of that application.

See Also Outlook Express Address Book

Perform Maintenance Tasks

1. Start the Outlook Express system by clicking once on the ![Start] button, then on **Programs, Internet Explorer, Outlook Express**.
2. Click on **File, Folder** and another subfolder will appear from which you can select the Compact Folders option.
3. After you arrive at the Compaction Area of Outlook Express, decide whether you want to compact just the folder you had highlighted (immediately before you accessed this menu tree) or if you want to compress all your Microsoft Outlook Express folders.

> **NOTE**
> It is suggested that you compress all the folders, regardless of which one(s) you did the last time you ran the compaction option(s). This will save you hard drive space by slimming-down the total file size of your Outlook Express data files. This is because when you delete an email message, the space that the message occupied is not automatically reclaimed. It takes the Compaction area to actually reclaim this space.

4. After you have completed the compaction process, click **View**, **Layout** to continue to the next maintenance task.

5. Make any choices you deem appropriate in the Window Layout Properties screen, and then continue to the next part of this configuration screen by clicking once on the `Customize Toolbar...` button.

6. Click once on an item in the left window and then click once on the `Add...` button to move it over to the right window (which means that it will now be shown on the Outlook Express toolbar).

> **TIP**
> One of my favorite selections is the Address Book, which lets you access the Outlook Express Address Book directly from the Outlook Express toolbar.

7. After you have made the selections you want, click once on the ✖ button to return to the previous page. From there, click once on the `OK` button to return to the primary Outlook Express screen.

8. To access the **Inbox Assistant**, select **Tools, Inbox Assistant** to reveal that screen.

> **NOTE**
> The Inbox Assistant is used to filter messages, perform automatic replies and forwards, move/copy messages to other specific Outlook Express folders, and perform specific server-side messaging functions.

9. To add one (or more) messaging rules, click once on the `Add...` button, as this will take you to the Properties window.

10. Use this window to define where the messages are originating that require a rule definition, and the bottom half of this window is where you define precisely what you want done to that message/specific group of messages/all messages. After you are done making your

selections, click once on the [OK] button to save your changes, activate them, and return to the main Inbox Assistant window (where you can view a descriptive listing of all your Inbox Assistant rules).

OUTLOOK EXPRESS NEWSGROUP READER

Configuring Microsoft Outlook Express for use with Internet newsgroups, such as those offered via your Internet service provider (ISP), is not a difficult task. An Internet account is required and should be provided by your ISP, or your organization's network administrator. (However, many companies do not permit access to Internet newsgroups via the corporate network through their firewall, so check with your network administrator first.) You then begin by using the configuration screens to create a new account (much like you did for an email account) for your Newsgroup connection. To help you through this process, try following these steps.

Configure Outlook Express Newsgroup Reader

1. Start the Outlook Express system by clicking once on the [Start] button, then select **Programs**, **Internet Explorer**, **Outlook Express**.

2. After the primary screen of the Outlook Express opens, look over to the left at the tree-like structure, which provides you with quick access to all the folders within the application: **Inbox**, **Outbox**, **Sent Items**, **Deleted Items**, and **Drafts**. (A draft is a message that you have composed and closed, but have not sent.) Choose **Tools, Accounts**.

3. The Internet Accounts window will appear. Click once on the **News** tab to be taken to that screen (the Internet Accounts windows will open with the **All** tab showing).

4. Click once on the [Add...] button to reveal a small menu, which contains three options: **Mail**, **News**, and **Directory Service** (all three of these menu selections

are used to create new mail, news, and/or directory service accounts). Click once on the **News** menu selection, which will reveal the next screen in the process.

5. On this first screen of the Internet Connection Wizard, you need to fill in the name that will appear whenever you post a message to a newsgroup.

> **NOTE**
>
> It is strongly recommended that you do not use your real name, much less your full name. Using an assumed name protects you and your privacy. Also, you might want to consider creating a dummy email address, such as "user@someplace.com," or something along that line of thinking.

6. After you have input the text that you want, click once on the [Next>] button to continue the process.

7. Here you need to enter the complete Internet email address that was assigned to you by your email administrator or Internet service provider (ISP). After you have input the text that you want, click once on the [Next>] button to continue the process.

8. Determine whether the Internet newsgroup account you are configuring requires you to logon to it or not (the vast majority of news servers do not). To use a logon ID and password with a **News Server**, click once on the check box near the bottom of the screen to select it (a check mark will appear in the box).

9. After you have input the name of the News Server, click once on the [Next>] button to continue the process.

10. If you did not request a News Server that requires logon information, this screen will not appear during your use of the Internet Connection Wizard. However, because we did request one, you need to click on one of the two radio buttons. The top one forces you to input essentially a user ID (it calls it a News Account Name) and a password. The bottom option uses the Secure Password Authentication option. In both cases, you must have been preassigned an account and password of some sort to use either of these two options correctly.

11. After you have input the necessary information, click once on the [Next>] button to continue the process.

12. On this screen, you need to create a descriptive name for your Internet News Account. This should be a name that will help you to remember exactly what is in this News Server's newsgroups. After you have input the friendly name, click once on the [Next>] button to continue the process.

13. You are prompted to select an **Internet Connection Type**. To choose one, click on the radio button next to the type that is required for you to connect your PC to the Internet. The top choice requires the use of a telephone, whereas the second one means that you are using a network connection, and the third one signifies that you do not want to change a selection that you already have in place (that is, you will need to manually establish your own connection each time you want to use the Outlook Express newsgroups).

14. After you have made your selection, click once on the [Next>] button to continue the process.

15. Review the information on this screen and then click once on the [Finish] button to end the wizard. This will return you to the Internet Accounts screen.

16. To complete the configuration process, click once on the [X] button to exit this screen. You will then find yourself in the main Outlook Express screen.

17. Next, ensure that you have already established a connection to the Internet.

18. Click once on your newsgroup account that you just made, and then click once on the **Newsgroups** icon that is found in the center of the top menu bar of this Outlook Express screen. This will take you into the Newsgroups screen.

> **NOTE**
>
> All of your News Servers accounts will appear in the column on the left, and their active newsgroups will appear in the center window area on the right. If there is a little newspaper icon to the left of a newsgroup's name, this means that you have already subscribed to that newsgroup. Otherwise, there is no icon, which means that the newsgroup has not yet been subscribed to. (You must first subscribe to a newsgroup before you can download and read its contents.)

19. Click on the newsgroup you want and click the **Subscriber** button. You may also double-click on any newsgroup, which will have the same effect: **Subscribed**.
20. To select all the newsgroups at once, click on the top one, and then while holding the ⇧Shift key down, go to the bottom of the list and click once on the bottom newsgroup. Then click the **Subscriber** button once.

> **NOTE**
>
> The **Unsubscribe** button does just that; it unsubscribes you from a newsgroup. The **Reset List** button will automatically reset the listing of newsgroups so that it becomes up-to-date with all the correct newsgroup names and descriptions.

21. After you have made all your selections, click once on the OK button to exit this screen.
22. Back on the main Outlook Express screen, click on any newsgroup in the left column to reveal its contents.
23. If you right-click on the name of a newsgroup in the left column, and then on **Properties** in the small pop-up menu that appears, you will be presented with the Properties screen for that particular newsgroup.

> **NOTE**
>
> Inside the various newsgroups in the left column, you will see a number inside a set of parentheses just to the right of each newsgroup name. This number is the total number of items that are contained within that newsgroup's discussion thread. However, this does not necessarily mean that you have already downloaded the contents of that entire newsgroup. For example, if you look in the right column, you might see that a message has been highlighted, but the contents appear to be missing. The statement `This message is not cached` means that you have not downloaded this newsgroup message. A quick way to determine whether a message has been downloaded yet is to examine its icon closely. If the icon appears to only be a tiny note with two lines of text (see the top message), then the full message has not been downloaded (only the header, which you are reading, has been downloaded).

24. The General tab appears, which gives you the full name of the newsgroup as well as the number of messages that are contained within it (including how many of these messages you have yet to read). As this is an informational screen only, there really is nothing to do here, so you might as well click once on the **Download** tab to continue on to that next screen. This is where you can specify how much information is automatically downloaded with each newsgroup.

25. Click once on the top check box to select it, which will then un-gray all the radio button options (thus making them available for selection). Then make your selection as to how much data you would like to download during a download session for this particular newsgroup.

26. After you have made your selection, click once on the **Local Files** tab to reveal the contents of that screen.

> **NOTE**
>
> The purpose of the Local Files tab is to help you minimize the amount of storage space a newsgroup occupies on your computer. As you read messages, download more, delete some, respond to others, and so on, you will create some wasted space on your PC that can only be reclaimed using a process known as compaction.

27. Click on the top button (Compact) to do just that. The **File Information** area at the top of this screen informs you of just how much space is being wasted by this newsgroup.
28. Click once on the Remove Messages button to delete all the message bodies that you have previously downloaded to your PC. This is helpful if you have not used this newsgroup in quite some time and want to just see the most recent information discussion threads.
29. Click once on the **Delete** button to delete all the messages (the headers as well as the bodies) that you have previously downloaded to your PC. This is useful if you have not used this newsgroup in quite some time and want to get a completely fresh start using it again.
30. Click once on the Reset button to restore the default information for this newsgroup. You can then download all the messages (this is like adding the newsgroup for the first time).
31. After you have made all your selections, click once on the OK button to close this screen and return to the primary Outlook Express screen.

> **NOTE**
>
> The remaining area that is of any importance for using newsgroups with the Outlook Express tool is the Tools menu. Use the **Tools** menu to access the **Accounts** area, to download a particular newsgroup or all them at once, as well as marking specific newsgroups for retrieval purposes (done during a Download All download session). Newsgroups can be filtered so that you do not see postings from particular individuals or messages that do not fall within a specific date range. The only special item on this menu is the **Get Next 1000 Headers** selection, which enables you to download the next thousand header messages for a particular newsgroup. (However, if you are downloading this many, you have way too much free time on your hands.)

See Also Dial-Up Networking

PAINT

The Microsoft Paint program enables you to view and slightly modify graphics files. Please keep in mind, however, that Paint permits you to create or modify just a few of the many different types of graphics files. Only the bitmap (*.bmp), GIF (*.gif), and JPEG (*.jpg & *.jpeg) file formats can be opened with Microsoft Paint. However, these three formats plus the monochrome (b/w), 16- and 256-color, and 24-bit bitmap file formats (*.bmp & *.dib) are acceptable forms in which to save Microsoft Paint files.

Use Paint

1. Click once on the **Start** button, then choose **Programs**, **Accessories**, and **Paint**, which will take you into the main Paint window.
2. To open an existing graphics file, click once on File and choose Open.
3. In the Open dialog, navigate to the file you want to open. Click on it once to select it, and then, click the **Open** button to reveal the file you selected inside the main Paint window.

Filler Tool

Paint Color Selection area

4. Paint provides many tools for modifying graphic files. For example, you can use the Fill tool to fill a selected area with any color you select from the color palette (along the bottom of the window).

5. To print a copy of your masterpiece, click once on the **File** menu and then choose **Print**. This will send a copy of your image to the default printer.

> **NOTE**
> One nice aspect of the Paint application is that it lets you undo your mistakes by either clicking on the Edit, Undo menu option or by using the Ctrl+Z keyboard combination. This enables you to play with this application on your favorite graphics files until you feel more comfortable using it, without having to worry about harming any existing picture file.

PASSWORDS

Think of a password as an electronic key. This key is a bit of information that is entered into a computer program to gain access to that particular application. There are many different kinds of passwords for Windows 98, such as those that enable you to access your organization's local and wide area networks, mainframes, as well as your local Windows 98 PC, and most of these can be altered from a single location. Keep in mind, though, that Windows 98 is not a secure operating system, and that anyone can click once on the **Esc** key to bypass the Windows 98 password to access your local PC's hard drive. This means that for that most part, Windows 98 passwords (in so much as the local PC, that is) do nothing to secure your own computer. They are really used by network operating systems that probably exist in most organizations today.

Change Passwords

1. Click once on the **Start** button, then choose **Settings, Control Panel**, which will take you into the Control Panel window.

2. Double-click on the **Passwords** icon in the Control Panel to access the **Change Passwords** tab of the Passwords Properties window. When you get there, click once on the [Change Windows Password...] button.

3. The Change Windows Password screen will appear. Type your old password (if this is the first time you are setting a password, leave this box blank), and then type your new password twice: once in the **New password** field and once in the **Confirm new password** field.

4. Click once on the [OK] button to accept the password change.

> **NOTE**
>
> You can change passwords such as those needed for the Windows NT network in the Other Passwords screen, which you reach by clicking the **Change Other Passwords button** in the **Change Passwords** tab of the Passwords Properties window.

5. Click once on the **Remote Administration** tab if you want to allow others to remotely manage your files and printers.

6. Click once on the **Enable Remote Administration of this Server** check box in this tab and then type the password that others will need to know to administer your PC remotely.

7. Click once on the **User Profiles** tab, if you want to be able to configure your computer for use by multiple users.

8. When you are finished changing the password options, click once on the [OK] button to confirm your changes and exit from this feature.

PC CARD (PCMCIA)

A PC Card, or PCMCIA (Personal Computer Manufacturers Card International Association) device, is a credit card-sized piece of hardware that enables specific functions on computers that support this option. PC Card slots are typically found only on laptop, notebook, and hand-held computing devices, but special drives can be installed on desktop PCs so that they are able to handle these types of devices. These devices are usually fax/modem, memory, and/or hard drive devices that are used to expand the functionality of the computers in which they are installed.

Windows 98 supports the Plug and Play features of countless numbers of these devices right out of the box, and many more through add-on software drivers. Double-click the **PCMCIA** icon in the Windows 98 **Control Panel** to verify settings for these devices.

PERSONAL WEB SERVER

The Windows 98 Personal Web Server is a wizard application that enables you to quickly create and display Web pages and sites on your own computer. You can also copy your Web site to another server (perhaps even your Internet service provider's so that it can be accessed via the Internet) for additional use.

Install the Personal Web Server

1. Insert the Windows 98 CD-ROM into your CD-ROM drive.
2. Click once on the [Start] button and then choose **Run**.
3. Type `D:\add-ins\pws\setup.exe` in the Run window where D: is referencing your CD drive letter. Then click once on the [OK] button to begin the installation process.

> **NOTE**
>
> Windows 98 provides instructions for installing the Personal Web Server. To view them, type `C:\windows\help\pws_main.htm` in the Run dialog used in the previous step.

4. The first installation screen will appear. Click once on the [Next>] button to continue.

5. The licensing agreement screen will now appear. Failure to accept the agreement will result in the termination of the installation process, so it is strongly advised that you click once on the **Accept** button. Click once on the `Next >` button to continue.

6. The next screen of the installation process will appear, where you will need to select the type of installation that best suits your needs. Although the **Typical** installation may work for you, you might want to try clicking once on the **Custom** option so that you can pick and choose exactly which components are installed on your computer. Then click once on the `Next >` button to continue.

7. The Microsoft Personal Web Server Setup screen lists all the components you can select to install (use the scrollbars to view the list in its entirety). Click the check box that corresponds with the components you want to install.

    Click once on the `Show Subcomponents...` button to view the subcomponents of the highlighted component. After you select all the features you want, click once on the `Next >` button to continue.

> **NOTE**
> If a component's corresponding check box is checked but grayed out, it indicates that not all of that component's subcomponents have been installed.

8. It is on the subcomponents screen where you can set or change the default folder destinations for any of the services on the screen. Enter the new folder path in the appropriate box and then click once on the `Next >` button to continue.

9. The next screen in the installation process is the one that enables you to specify where the **Microsoft Transaction Server** will be installed. Either accept the default location or change it to one that better meets your needs, and then click once on the `Next >` button to continue.

10. The progress bar shown keeps track of the installation's progress. When the installation is complete, click once on the [Next>] button to continue.

11. The **Personal Web Server** installation process is now complete. Click once on the [Finish] button to end the process.

12. You will now be prompted to restart your computer, which you should do by clicking once on the [Yes] button.

Use Personal Web Server After Installation

1. Double-click the **Publish** icon that now appears on your desktop to access the **Personal Web Server** application.

2. The Tip of the Day window appears. Either click once on the [Next>] button to view another tip or click once on the [X] button to exit the Tip of the Day dialog.

> **NOTE**
> To prevent this dialog from appearing each time you start the **Personal Web Server**, uncheck the **Show Tips at Startup** check box.

3. If you clicked the [X] button in the previous step, the Personal Web Manager screen will now appear. From here, you can fully manage your Web site, including creating new pages through the **Publish Wizard**. It is suggested that you play with the various options found within this screen to become more familiar with them, as there are whole books that cover the ins-and-outs of Web site creation.

PHONE DIALER

The Windows 98 Phone Dialer enables you to make telephone calls from your computer by using your modem or another Windows telephone device.

Use Phone Dialer

1. Click once on the [Start] button, then choose **Programs, Accessories, Communications**, and then **Phone Dialer**.
2. The Phone Dialer screen opens. Determine what hardware this application will connect to place calls. To do this, click once on **Tools** and then select **Connect Using**. This opens the Connect Using screen.
3. Specify the hardware device (such as a modem) to be used in the **Line** drop-down list box.
4. To modify how telephone calls are to be made (refer to the section on Dial-Up Networking for further details on this option), click once on the [Line Properties...] button to open the Modem Name Properties window. Also use this screen to modify the properties of the modem that has been selected, and then click once on the [OK] button to return to the main Phone Dialer screen.
5. Chose **Tools, Dialing Properties**.
6. The Dialing Properties screen opens. Specify or modify information about the location from which you are dialing.
7. Click once on the [OK] button to return to the main Phone Dialer screen.

See Also Dial-Up Networking

Add Recipients to Your Speed Dial List

1. In the main Phone Dialer window, click once on **Edit** and then on **Speed Dial**. This will open the Edit Speed Dial screen.
2. Type the name of the person you want to add in the **Name** field.
3. Enter the person's telephone number in the **Number to Dial** field.
4. Repeat these steps for any other people you want to add to the speed dial area.

5. Click once on the `Save` button to return to the Phone Dialer screen.

6. To place a call using speed dial, click the button labeled with the name of the person you want to call.

> **NOTE**
>
> To place a call without using the speed dial feature, enter the complete telephone number (with area code, if going outside your normal calling area) in the box just below the label **Number to Dial:** (the box is located just above the `Dial` button). You do this by either typing in the numbers using the keypad on your computer's keyboard or by clicking on each number on the number keypad provided just below the `Dial` button. After you have typed-in the telephone number, click once on the `Dial` button to start the call. That is all there is to it!

See Also Telephony Properties

POWER MANAGEMENT

The Windows 98 power management feature helps you conserve energy by reducing the power consumption needs of your computing devices. This feature functions by letting you create a power scheme—essentially a series of settings that manages your PC's power needs. For example, you can configure your PC to save power by automatically turning off the system monitor or stopping the hard drive after a preset period of idle time.

Configure Power Management

1. Click once on the `Start` button, then choose **Settings**, and then **Control Panel**, which will take you into the Control Panel window.

2. Double-click the **Power Management** icon in the Control Panel window.

3. The **Power Schemes** tab of the Power Management Properties screen appears. Click the down-arrow button to the right of the **Power Schemes** field to view a drop-down list box containing the three available sample power management schemes.

4. Choose the power scheme that best describes your work environment, and then set the time limits at the bottom of the screen.

5. Click once on the **Advanced** tab to view that screen. Here you can select whether you want to show the power meter on the taskbar and whether you want to be prompted for a password when the computer goes off standby mode.

6. Click once on the [OK] button to save your changes.

PRINTERS

A basic but important need of any Windows 98 user is the capability to print information from his or her computer. To do this, you must first have a physical printer, and second be able to install the proper software drivers for your locally connected printer (assuming you have one). After your printer is installed, click once on the [Start] button, then **Settings**, **Printers** to open the Printers window. Take a closer look at the printer(s) that are available for use with your computer.

The printer that has a check mark (inside a black or dark circle) next to it is the default printer for your PC. This means that whenever you go to print from inside a Windows 98 application, such as your word processor, your document will automatically go to this default printer. When you are getting ready to print something, you will usually be presented with an option to **Preview** your potential output. What this does, is to give you the chance to see exactly what your printed document will look like before you actually print it. This way you are able to save a few extra trees by not printing something that has a glaring mistake in it.

See Also Add a Printer Wizard

PRODIGY INTERNET

Prodigy Internet is one of the online services (AOL, AT&T WorldNet Service, CompuServe, and Microsoft Network are the others) that is available for installation as part of the Windows 98 operating system. When Windows 98 is installed, pointers to these five services are installed in order to ensure the availability of the software for these services. Like the other online services (except for Microsoft Network) that are available, Prodigy Internet is readily installed from within the online services folder found on the main Windows 98 Desktop.

Install and Sign Up for Prodigy Internet

Open the **Online Services** folder and double-click the **Prodigy Internet** service to begin the installation process. Follow the remaining Prodigy Internet installation prompts. Upon completion, you will be required to restart your PC. Do so to complete the installation process. When your computer finishes restarting, you will see a new shortcut on your Windows 98 Desktop. Double-click on that icon to start using the Prodigy Internet online service.

See Also America Online (AOL), AT&T WorldNet Service, CompuServe, and Microsoft Network

QUICK LAUNCH

Windows 98 has several toolbars that have been added since previous Windows versions. A good example is the Quick Launch toolbar, which automatically sets up links or shortcuts to key features such as the Windows 98 Desktop, Outlook Express, Internet Channels, and the Microsoft Internet Explorer browser, just to name a few. You can find the Quick Launch area to the right of the Start button on the taskbar.

You can place additional shortcut icons on the Quick Launch toolbar simply by clicking the shortcut you want to add, and dragging it to the Quick Launch area (it will automatically insert itself on the toolbar).

See Also Toolbars

QUICK VIEW

To quickly view the contents of a file, you can use the Windows 98 utility known as *Quick View*. To use Quick View, first navigate to the file you want to view (for more information on navigation in Windows 98, see the Windows Explorer section in this book). After you have found the file you want, right-click on it once and then select the **Quick View** option from the shortcut menu. The file you selected opens inside the Quick View application.

RESTARTING WINDOWS 98

Restart is just the geek-speak way of saying that you will be restarting your Windows 98-computer system. So, when Windows 98 prompts you to restart your system, it just means that you need to shut it down and restart it.

Restart Windows 98

1. Click once on the **Start** button and then choose the **Shut Down** menu selection.
2. The Shut Down Windows screen appears. Click once on the **Restart** radio button, and then click once on the **OK** button to begin the restart process.

> **NOTE**
> Whichever radio button you selected the last time you shut down your computer will be selected by default (if this is the first time you've used this screen, the top option will be selected).

RECYCLE BIN

When a file or folder is deleted from your computer, it first goes to the **Recycle Bin** found on the Windows 98 Desktop.

> **NOTE**
> When the Recycle Bin contains no files or folders, the **Recycle Bin** icon shown on the desktop appears to be empty. When you place files or folders in the Recycle Bin, the **Recycle Bin** icon appears to be stuffed with paper (assuming, of course, that you have not altered the graphical icon for your **Recycle Bin**).

To view the contents of the **Recycle Bin**, double-click its icon on the desktop. If you decide that you no longer wish to delete a file or folder that you have placed in the **Recycle Bin**, simply right-click the file and choose **Restore** from the shortcut menu. This returns the file or folder to the location where it resided before you attempted to delete it.

> **NOTE**
>
> If you do not see the **Recycle Bin** icon on your desktop, it is probably just hiding behind one of your open folders or applications. Try right-clicking a blank area of the taskbar and choosing **Minimize All Windows**; the **Recycle Bin** icon should then reveal itself to you.

Empty the Recycle Bin

1. Right-click the **Recycle Bin** icon and choose **Empty Recycle Bin** from the shortcut menu.

2. A window will appear that verifies that you are certain you want to delete the contents of the **Recycle Bin**. If you are certain, click once on the [Yes] button.

> **NOTE**
>
> If the Recycle Bin contains only one file, the dialog shown will provide the name of the file to be deleted. If the Recycle Bin contains multiple files, the dialog will simply tell you how many files will be deleted.

3. Upon your return to the Windows 98 Desktop, you will notice that the Recycle Bin icon no longer appears to be stuffed with paper.

REGIONAL SETTINGS PROPERTIES

Windows 98's Regional Settings feature makes it much easier to change the default time, date, currency, and number configurations for your PC.

Configure Regional Settings Properties

1. Click once on the [Start] button, then choose **Settings**, **Control Panel** to open the Control Panel window.

2. Double-click the **Regional Settings** icon in the Control Panel window to access that window.

3. The **Regional Settings** tab of the Regional Settings Properties dialog appears. Depending on where you live, such as Chicago (or anywhere else in the United States

of America), you may want to leave the default option of **English (United States)** selected. However, since quite a few Windows 98 users reside outside of the USA, you may want to select a different language (such as British English, Russian, Slovak, Polish, or Macedonian, to name a few). To do that, click on the down-arrow button next to the text field and click the language you want to use.

> **NOTE**
> You might be prompted to restart your computer immediately following a language change. Click [Yes], and restart before changing additional regional settings.

4. Click once on the **Number** tab to access the screen where you can specify exactly how numbers and decimal points are configured for your local environment.

5. Click once on the **Currency** tab to access the screen where you are able to specify how currency figures are to be configured for your local environment.

6. Click once on the **Time** tab to open the screen where you can select the format of the system clock.

7. Click once on the **Date** tab to access the screen where you can select the format of the local calendar and date type, as well as specify any Year 2000 system settings.

8. Click once on the [OK] button to accept your changes and return to the Windows 98 Desktop.

See Also Year 2000

REGISTRATION PROCESS FOR WINDOWS 98

After you have installed Windows 98 (or have acquired a PC that came with Windows 98 pre-installed), you should register the operating system software with Microsoft. If you register Windows 98, you become eligible for product support as well as ensure that you will be made aware of any future product enhancements.

Register Windows 98

1. Connect to the Internet.
2. Click once on the [Start] button, then choose **Programs, Accessories, System Tools,** and **Welcome to Windows.**
3. Click once on the **Register Now** entry shown in the **Contents** menu of the Welcome to Windows 98 screen.
4. The first screen of the Registration Wizard explains to you the benefits of registering your copy of Windows 98. To continue the registration process, click once on the [Next>] button.
5. The next screen of the wizard informs you that the **Registration Wizard** is about to inventory your system's hardware. Click once on the [Next>] button to continue.

> **NOTE**
>
> Do not panic! Microsoft is not stealing information from your PC, nor is it gathering bits of information about competitive products that you might be using. This is simply a harmless information-gathering procedure to help Microsoft customer support should you require assistance somewhere down the road. Microsoft is not acquiring nearly as much information as your hardware vendor already has stuffed in a database somewhere about you and your computing preferences. However, Microsoft has issued a software patch that will prevent the unauthorized sending of your unique user information to them without your permission (to get this patch, refer to the Microsoft Web site found at this URL: http://www.Microsoft.com/).

6. In the next screen of the wizard, type in your first name, last name, and company name (type your company's name only if your employer—not you—purchased this version of Windows 98). Click once on the [Next>] button to continue.
7. In this next screen, enter your address information, including country.

> **NOTE**
> If you provide an email address, Microsoft will occasionally send you electronic messages informing you of changes to the product.

8. Click once on the `Next>` button to continue.
9. Here you can specify where you bought Windows 98 and whether you want to be included in various offers of non-Microsoft products and services (these are optional choices). Make your selections and/or entries, and then click once on the `Next>` button to continue.
10. If you decide to forward this information to Microsoft, then click on the **Yes** radio button. Otherwise, click on the **No** radio button to decline, and then click once on the `Next>` button to continue.
11. Write down the Windows 98 product ID number that appears in the middle of the informational screen (this number is unique to your computer, and will be required should you ever need product support from Microsoft). Click once on the `Register` button to start the actual registration communication process.
12. You will see a message box informing you that your registration information is being sent to Microsoft. After the registration process is complete, you will see a confirmation dialog appear. Click once on the `Finish` button to complete the process.
13. You are returned to the Welcome to Windows 98 screen, where you will notice that the **Register Now** entry has a check mark to the right of it. This indicates that you have successfully completed the Windows 98 registration process. Click once on the × button in the upper-right corner of the screen to close this window.

See Also Windows Update

REGISTRY

The Windows 98 Registry is the logical database that contains all the critical, and sometimes dynamic, information regarding your Windows 98 operating system implementation. Think of the Registry as the center of the Windows 98 universe, much like the sun is to the earth. Without the sun, everything on Earth dies...without the Registry, Windows 98 is dead in the water. You might want to review Jerry Honeycutt's book *Using the Windows 98 Registry* (Que Corporation, 1998).

> **WARNING**
> The Windows 98 Registry is a dangerous place for beginners or relatively inexperienced Windows 98 users! This cannot be stressed enough! One mistake, and you might cause your computer to stop working without any chance for a do-over or a mulligan. Keep this in mind whenever you make a modification to the Windows 98 Registry.

Although the Registry is almost always referred to as single data store, you should really understand that the Registry consists of three files: USER.DAT, SYSTEM.DAT, and POLICY.POL. The first two files are initially stored in the primary Windows folder (usually C:\Windows), whereas the latter one can be found in the same place or in one of the Windows subfolders.

The USER.DAT file contains the user-specific information for your Windows 98 installation. It holds the information that a typical user would change on her computer, such as the desktop configuration colors; logon profiles, including the user name; and the changeable Windows 98 folder structure that exists on the Start menu. Although on a single user environment this file is important, as soon as you start putting several users on the same Windows 98 workstation (such as in a call-center operation or on a corporate-controlled network), it becomes a vital file to managing user information. If there are multiple users on the same PC, this file will be stored in the *windir*\Profiles*username* folder (where *windir* equates to the location of the Windows 98 installation; and *username* will equal the logon profile name for each user). If you are connected to a network, then this file might well be stored on your local file server and not on your Windows 98 PC.

The SYSTEM.DAT file stores the computer-specific the hardware information for your Windows 98 computer. It contains information such as IRQ (hardware interrupt) settings, the Plug and Play enumerations, application-specific data, and network configurations. This file is always found in the Windows root folder (typically C:\Windows), and is stored as a hidden, read-only file. This is by far the single, most critical Windows 98 system file. Lose it, delete it, or corrupt it, and your system will most certainly be in a world of hurt (imagine someone losing, deleting, or damaging your heart, and you will understand what this file means to the Windows 98 "body").

The POLICY.POL Registry file is actually an optional one. It does not have to exist for Windows 98 to function properly, nor will its accidental corruption or deletion crash your Windows 98 implementation. What the POLICY.POL file does for you is to store Windows-specific information that automatically overrides any information stored in the USER.DAT or SYSTEM.DAT Registry files. Thus, in a sense, the POLICY.POL file is a Windows 98 security file. It contains specific information that your network administrator uses to better manage the multitude of computers across the company's networks, while providing some sense of security to the local Windows 98 user. Now, in reality, you probably already know that Windows 98 will probably never be viewed as a "secure" operating system; additionally, the alteration of the POLICY.POL file is probably beyond the average user. For added security, it is recommended that this file be stored on a Windows NT 4.0 Server (or Windows 2000 Server, Advanced Server, or DataCenter), which is forced down to each user (in background, of course) whenever they log on to the network. This way, even if someone alters their local version of this file, a new one would override the changed version the next time they logged on to the corporate network systems.

In many ways, the Windows 98 Registry resembles a collection of *.INI initialization files. This is because many 16-bit and almost all 32-bit applications store their configuration data in the Registry instead of the old Windows 3.x-style initialization files that have an .INI file extension. In addition, the Registry keys can be imported and exported at will, which means you can edit those keys with a common text editor such as the Windows Notepad the same way you edit an .INI file.

The Windows 98 Registry architecture has not really changed much from its Windows 95 counterpart. It has a few more keys for items that did not exist in Windows 95, such as those for WebTV for Windows, WBEM, the Version Conflict Manager, and so on. However, for the most part, you will find the Registry organized much the same way in Windows 98. It has the same the key structure, with the same six Registry hives:

- HKEY_CLASSES_ROOT
- HKEY_CURRENT_USER
- HKEY_LOCAL_MACHINE
- HKEY_USERS
- HKEY_CURRENT_CONFIG
- HKEY_DYN_DATA

Additionally, these hives are all edited directly with the Windows Registry Editor tool known as REGEDIT.EXE (found in the local Windows root folder).

The HKEY_CLASSES_ROOT Registry section the is used to store important object linking and embedding (OLE) information, which tells the operating system how to handle its drag-and-drop operations as well as its system links. This section is actually a pointer to the Registry key setting of the HKEY_LOCAL_MACHINE\Software\Classes section of the Windows 98 Registry.

> **NOTE**
>
> Windows 98 is different from Windows 95 in two primary ways. First, you are no longer limited by the 65,536-byte limit for a single Registry key. What this means is that now, for the first time, it becomes realistic to store and use more applications that use shared dynamic link library (DLL) files (a DLL file contains programming information that is vital to the execution of a particular Windows 98 application). Look in the \Windows\System subfolder to find most of the DLL files on your computer. This is an improvement for Windows 98 users because it permits applications to share more files among them and should cut down on the useless redundancy of too many files on your PC. The other difference is in the way that the Windows 98 operating system handles the Registry, including its self-healing aspects (for example, the Registry can automatically find its own problems and fix them without human intervention).

The HKEY_CURRENT_USER portion of the Registry holds user-specific configuration data for the user that is presently logged on to the Windows 98 PC, and is actually a pointer to the specific branch in the HKEY_USERS for that user.

The HKEY_LOCAL_MACHINE Registry hive contains the hardware details for your computer. This is an important hive, and is the one that you will find yourself in 80 percent of the time, changing and tweaking tiny aspects of your system to make it work better.

The HKEY_USERS Registry hive is similar to the HKEY_CURRENT_USER section, except that the HKEY_USERS hive holds the data for all registered users of this installation of Windows 98.

The HKEY_CURRENT_CONFIG key is similar to the HKEY_LOCAL_MACHINE hive, except that it only contains information regarding the hardware configuration of your PC during this session.

The last hive, HKEY_DYN_DATA, holds all the dynamic data for the various system devices such as your modem, tape drive, or monitor. The current status of each hardware device is tracked in this section of the Windows 98 Registry, and it contains sub-keys for every additional user that might log on to your PC at some time.

Now that you have sufficient background to work in your Registry, it is time to get started. Remember, however, that the Registry is a fragile item that is very unforgiving should you make a mistake or delete something you should not have. Although the direct editing of the Registry is a powerful aspect of using Windows 98, any error here, no matter how small, can spell disaster for your computer system!

RESOURCE METER

You can use the Windows 98 Resource Meter to monitor the health of your computer system by displaying how much of your system's resources are available.

Run the Resource Meter

1. Click once on the **Start** button, then choose **Programs**, **Accessories**, **System Tools**, and **Resource Meter**.

2. Read the informational box that appears and then click once on the **OK** button to continue. Click the **Don't Display this Message Again** check box if you do not want to be bothered with this dialog again.

> **NOTE**
> To avoid draining system resources unnecessarily, run the Resource Meter only when you need to know how much of your system's resources are available.

3. You will return to the Windows 98 Desktop. In the far-right portion of the taskbar, you will see an icon that represents the **Resource Meter**. If you hover your mouse pointer over this icon, you can view what percentages of the following resources are free:

    - **System**—A system resource is a function of the operating system that is required by Windows 98 and will usually be present. There is not much tuning or tweaking you can do to increase this number (other than to eliminate some Windows 98 features and functions).

- **User**—User resources are those resources that are consumed by the use of backgrounds, the addition of icons and HTML files to the desktop, the simultaneous opening of several programs, and so on.
- **GDI**—GDI resources are those resources that are consumed by the graphics capabilities of your PC. To decrease the consumption of GDI resources, you might reduce the number of colors your monitor shows from High (either 24 bit, which equates to 16.7 million colors; or 16 bit, which equates to 65,000 colors) to 256.

4. If you have trouble seeing the percentages on the desktop, right-click the **Resource Meter** icon, and then choose **Details** from the shortcut menu.
5. After you have finished examining the contents of the Resource Meter, click once on [OK] button to close it.

RUN...

The Windows 98 Run window enables you to execute run commands to start programs or open folders, documents, or Internet resources.

Use the Run Window

1. Click once on the [Start] button and choose **Run**.
2. In the Run window, type the full path to the program executable file you want to run (if you do not know the full path, then click once on the [Browse...] button to find the file).

SCANDISK

ScanDisk is used for examining and repairing problems with the file and folder structure on your hard drive.

Use ScanDisk

1. Click once on the [Start] button; select **Programs, Accessories, System Tools,** and **ScanDisk**.
2. Click once on the [Advanced...] button in the ScanDisk window to access the ScanDisk Advanced Options screen.
3. Select the check boxes and the radio buttons for the options you want, and click once on the [OK] button to return to the main screen.
   - **Display Summary**—This option shows you a summary of your scan.
   - **Log File**—This option keeps a history file of your scan.
   - **Cross-Linked Files**—This option determines how to handle files that are linked to more than one program because they have the same name.
   - **Lost File Fragments**—This option determines how to handle fragments of files that remain on your system.
   - **Check File For**—This option search for either Invalid names and/or Invalid dates because these errors can lead to cross-linking.
   - **Check Host Drive First**—This option always checks your main hard drive first.
4. Select the hard drive that you want scanned (you can select multiple drives by shift-clicking the drives you want).
5. Choose either a Standard (error checks files and folders only) or a Thorough (also checks disk surface) scan.

6. If you choose Thorough, you can select additional options for the disk surface scan by clicking on [Options...]. After you make your selections, click [OK] to return to the main Scandisk window.

7. Click once on [Start] to run the ScanDisk application for the highlighted hard drive. You will be notified when the program finishes.

See Also Maintenance Wizard, Scheduled Task Manager

SCHEDULED TASKS MANAGER

The Windows 98 Scheduled Tasks Manager enables you to schedule tasks, such as ScanDisk, at whatever time you specify. The Scheduled Tasks Manager starts every time Windows 98 starts, and is present in the background system memory as a TSR program (terminate-and-stay resident). When the Scheduled Tasks Manager is operational, its icon appears on the taskbar near the clock.

> **NOTE**
> If you hover the mouse pointer over the **Scheduled Tasks Manager** icon, a tiny message box appears, showing the status of the Scheduled Tasks Manager application.

Add a Task to Scheduled Tasks Manager

1. Click on [Start], **Programs, Accessories, System, Add Scheduled Task Wizard**.

2. Double-click the **Add Scheduled Task** icon to start the wizard. Its first screen contains information about adding tasks. Click once on the [Next >] button to continue.

3. Select an application from the Application list. This list contains all applications that have been registered with the Windows 98 operating system, but you can always click the [Browse...] button to locate applications that are not present in the list. Click [Next >].

4. Type a descriptive name for the task (the name shown in the main Task Scheduler window). Select how often you want this task performed from the radio buttons, and click [Next >] to continue.

5. Specify the time and day you want the task to start, and click [Next >].

6. Click once the check box if you want to view or modify the Advanced Properties screen for your selected task. (Most applications have different types of advanced properties, so read the prompts carefully for each task.)

7. Click [Finish] to complete the process and return to the Scheduled Tasks screen. Your new task will now appear in the window.

8. To run your task immediately, right-click the task and select the **Run** option.

See Also Disk Defragmenter, Maintenance Wizard, ScanDisk

SCREEN SAVER

Screen savers provide a series of graphics that hide the application open on your computer. The original purpose of a screen saver was to help prevent screen *burn-in*, in which a faint image of your screen's former contents remained visible even after you turned off your monitor or moved to new contents. Although some people still use screen savers for this purpose, in most cases they are used only for their entertainment value.

Choose a Screen Saver

1. Right-click on a blank portion of the desktop and then choose the **Properties** menu selection from the small pop-up menu that appears.

2. Click once on the **Screen Saver** tab in the Display Properties window to access that tab's contents.

3. Click on the down-arrow button to the right of the **Screen Saver** field and select a screen saver from the drop-down list.

4. To set the options for a specific screen saver, click once on the `Settings...` button to view that screen saver's **Options** area.

5. After you set your screen savers options, click once on the `OK` button to return to the **Screen Saver** tab of the Display Properties dialog.

6. Click once on the `Preview` button to view a full-screen preview of the screen saver, and then click or move the mouse to end the preview session.

7. To password-protect the screen saver, check the **Password Protected** check box. Then click once on the `Change...` button. This opens the Change Password screen.

8. If you have never added a password to a screen saver, you will be prompted to enter and confirm the new password. Otherwise, you will need to know the original password before you can change it to a new one. Fill in the text fields as needed.

9. Click once on the `OK` button to return to the Display Properties screen, and then click once on the `OK` button again to accept all changes and return to the desktop.

SHORTCUTS: CREATE, DELETE, AND MODIFY

A shortcut, as the name suggests, is a feature that lets you shorten the steps to opening your applications, documents, and other files. This Windows 98 feature—also known as a *link*—permits you to access a file or application without having to navigate through all of the menus or folders that would normally be required. The shortcut is in essence a file that simply jumps the computer to another file or program on your hard drive. You can give the shortcuts a graphical appearance to help you identify them and because they are so small (usually only 1KB) you can have as many of them as you like. Just create a shortcut anywhere that you might expect to want to jump to a file or program quickly, such as a briefcase, desktop, or work folder.

Create a Shortcut from Scratch

1. Right-click any blank spot on the desktop, and, in the shortcut menu that appears, choose **New, Shortcut**.
2. The **Create Shortcut Wizard** starts. In the first screen, either type the full path including the target file for your shortcut or click once on the `Browse...` button to find the file on your computer. Click once on the `Next >` button to continue.
3. At the Select a Title for the Program screen, type a descriptive name for your shortcut (this is the name you will see on the desktop).
4. Click once on the `Finish` button to complete the wizard and return to the desktop. The newly created shortcut can now be seen on your desktop.

Rename a Shortcut

1. Right-click a shortcut and choose **Properties** from the shortcut menu.
2. The Properties window for the shortcut you have selected opens.
3. Click the **Shortcut** tab of the Properties window, and then click once on the `Change Icon...` button to alter the shortcut's icon.
4. Select the icon you want to use or click the `Browse...` button to find other icons. After you have clicked once on the icon you want, click `OK`.

> **NOTE**
>
> In most cases, the shortcut, by default, will be assigned a predetermined icon (one that came with the program). In others, just before the last step in the creation process, the Select an Icon window will appear. Just click on the picture of your choice and then click on the `Finish` button to confirm your choice.

5. To accept changes and exit, click once on the `OK` button in the Properties screen.

Delete a Shortcut

Click on the shortcut icon that you want to delete, and then either drag it over to the Windows 98 Recycle Bin or just press the Del key on your computer's keyboard. Either way the shortcut will be moved to the Recycle Bin.

Rename a Shortcut

Right-click on the shortcut you want to rename, and click once on the Rename option. The name of the shortcut will be highlighted, and you will now be able to type in anything you want (that is considered a valid keystroke) as your new shortcut's name.

See Also Desktop, Desktop Themes

SHUT DOWN WINDOWS 98

Because Windows 98 performs so many tasks in the background, including caching memory before saving it, it is imperative that you turn off your PC in a structured manner. If you were to simply cut the power to your PC, you might lose data that you thought you had already saved to the hard drive.

Shut Down Windows

1. Close any open applications, and click Start, **Shut Down**.

2. Select the **Shut down** radio button in the Shut Down Windows screen, and then click once on the OK button.

3. Your computer will automatically shut itself down and, if your computer's internal BIOS supports this, power itself off (most laptop and newer desktop PCs support this feature). Otherwise, you will see a full screen message saying that "It is now safe to turn off your computer." In which case, simply push the power button on your computer's CPU (Computer Processing Unit).

SOUND PROPERTIES

Sound Properties is the way that Windows lets you control the sound made by your computer for various program events. This allows you to create your own personalized computing experience. This feature can also be used with Desktop Themes to create sounds that are related to a common theme.

Change a Sound Property

1. Click once on the [Start] button, then choose **Settings, Control Panel**.
2. When the Windows 98 Control Panel window appears, double-click on the **Sounds** icon, to reveal the Sound Properties screen.
3. Select the program event in the **Events** window that you want to change. Events that have speaker icons to the left of them currently have a sound applied to them.

> **NOTE**
>
> You will notice that aside from Windows and its components, which are the first programs listed, the rest of the applications are in alphabetical order. In addition, only certain programs have unique events that you can modify. In most cases, the overall system settings will apply within these other applications.

4. The current sound information will be displayed in the **Sound** area of this screen. To listen to the current sound, click the ▶ button in the **Preview** area.
5. To change the sound file, select another sound from the Name drop-down list or click [Browse...] to navigate to another sound file.
6. Click the ▶ button to listen to the selected sound.
7. Alternatively, you can click the down-arrow button next to the **Scheme** text box to select an overall system-wide sound scheme.

8. If you do select a **Scheme** for your computer, you might be asked to save your existing sound options as a scheme so that you can go back to them at some point. Enter a **Name** in the text box and click [OK].

9. Click [OK] after you have made your changes. If you have changed your mind, click [Cancel] to restore your previous settings.

See Also Desktop Themes

START MENU

The Windows 98 Start menu consists of all those menu options that appear above the [Start] button: **Run**, **Help**, **Find**, **Settings**, **Documents**, **Favorites**, **Programs**, and any shortcuts that you might have added.

Add Programs to the Start Menu

Click on the file or shortcut that you want to appear on your Start Menu (these can be in a folder, on the desktop, in Windows Explorer, and so on), and simply drag the icon of the file or application you want to the Start Menu. Click [Start] and choose **Settings**, **Taskbar**.

Delete an Item from the Start Menu

1. Click once on the [Start] button, and choose **Settings**, **Taskbar**.

2. Choose the **Start Menu Programs** tab and select [Remove].

3. Locate the shortcut in the Explorer style window of the Start Menu folder, and click on it once to select it.

4. Click the [Remove] button, and click [Yes] to confirm that you want the shortcut removed to the Recycle Bin.

5. After you have removed all the unwanted shortcuts, click ☒ to return to the **Start Menu Programs** tab.

> **NOTE**
>
> If you want to really get in there and organize your Start Menu shortcuts, simply click [Advanced...] on the Start Menu Programs tab. This will take you to a Windows Explorer Start Menu window. Here you can add, remove, rename, and rearrange the shortcuts just as you can within Windows Explorer.

See Also My Computer, Windows Explorer

START WINDOWS 98

Starting the Windows 98 operating system is simple:

1. Remove any floppies and/or CDs from their drives and turn your PC on.

2. It will take a few seconds but it should eventually appear at the Windows 98 Desktop. You might be presented with a Welcome to Windows password box. Enter your User name and Password and press [↵Enter] on your keyboard. If you do not want to use a password you can either press the [Esc] key on your keyboard or click [Cancel].

3. Any programs or utilities that are listed in your C:/Windows/Start Menu/Programs/Startup folder will automatically initialize. After they have stopped you will be at your desktop and ready to work.

See Also Desktop, Start Menu, Windows Explorer

SYSTEM PROPERTIES

The system properties screens of Windows 98 provide raw information about the hardware installed on your computer system, and a starting point for troubleshooting hardware configurations gone wrong.

> **WARNING**
> If you incorrectly make changes on any of these screens, you can mess things up in such a way that reinstalling the Windows 98 operating system is your only hope for recovery.

To use the System Properties screens, right-click the **My Computer** icon on the desktop, and choose **Properties** from the shortcut menu that appears.

The System Properties screen contains several tabs:

- **General**—This informational tab contains information about your system, including how much memory you have installed in your PC.
- **Device Manager**—This tab shows all the installed hardware devices and their connection points.

> **NOTE**
> If an icon is overlapped with a black exclamation point in a yellow circle, it indicates that the Windows 98 believes that there is a problem with the hardware device represented. Whether it's right or wrong, you should investigate any of these occurrences.

- **Hardware Profiles**—This screen enables you to create separate start up profiles for your hardware devices. For example, suppose you use a notebook computer. When you are at work, it plugs into a docking station with network cards, modems, and the like. When you are at home, it sits on a table with a separate monitor, keyboard, mouse, and Yamaha sound system connected into it. Keeping track of all these hardware devices in a single configuration would drive you mad. Using the **Hardware Profiles** tab, you can create separate hardware configuration schemes; this is similar to the multiple start up options that many people had under DOS 6.*x*.
- **Performance**—The top area of this tab is for informational purposes; the three buttons along the bottom—**File System, Graphics,** and **Virtual Memory**—enable you to modify key elements of your computer system.

> **NOTE**
>
> If you do not completely understand what you are doing in the **File System**, **Graphics**, and **Virtual Memory** areas, stay with the settings that the Windows 98 operating system installed for you (they are probably adequate). Failure to make the correct selections, which will vary from PC to PC, can cause intermittent computer system deficiencies.

SYSTEM FILE CHECKER

Windows 98 provides a utility known as the System File Checker. The System File Checker is one of the tools started from inside the **Microsoft System Information** tool, or it can be started directly from the Windows 98 **Run** command box. The purpose of the System File Checker is to scan your important system files and figure out which ones have been altered since you installed Windows 98. Altered files could lead to lost data or system crashes in the future. It will also determine whether any of them have been corrupted, and will then offer to restore any of those corrupted files from backup copies that Windows 98 automatically preserves for you elsewhere on your PC.

Use System File Checker

1. Click [Start], then choose **Programs, Accessories, System Tools, System Information**.
2. Choose **Tools, System File Checker**.

> **TIP**
>
> You can also start the System File Checker by clicking [Start] and choosing **Run**. Type in the `SFC.exe` command, and click the [OK] button (or press the [Enter] key).

3. Click once on the [Settings...] button, to configure System File Checker utility options more to your liking.

> **NOTE**
>
> The **Settings** tab lets you control the location for file backups, the restore file prompt setting, the log file options, and it gives you the ability to check for changed and/or deleted system files. These last two options are probably the most powerful ones on this screen. If you enable both of these options, the System File Checker utility will look not only at corrupted system files but also at ones that have been deleted or changed (its CRC has been altered) in any way.

4. To change the location of the backup files, click once on the Change... button and select a new locale.
5. To view an existing log file (that is, a log from a previous use of the System File Checker utility), click once on the View Log button.
6. Click once on the **Search Criteria** tab, and choose the options you want.

> **NOTE**
>
> The Search Criteria screen lets you modify the manner in which the System File Checker utility scans your PC. The default set of system folders to be scanned is provided for you, but you may modify them. You may also change the system file types, either adding or removing file types.

7. If you require your system configuration files to be restored to the original, click once on the **Advanced** tab.
8. Click once on the **Restore Defaults** button to perform a restoration of your system's default configuration file (Default.sfc).

> **NOTE**
>
> The purpose of the Restore Defaults option is to create a new default system configuration file if yours has become corrupted or was deleted. This option will restore all of your computer's configuration files to the original Windows 98 installation settings.

9. After you have finished making your alterations to the System File Checker Settings screens, click once on the `OK` button to accept your changes. This will return you to the primary screen of the System File Checker utility.

> **NOTE**
>
> System File Checker main screen has two important options. The top radio button allows your Windows 98 to perform a scan on your computer for altered system files (you will be prompted to perform restores where needed). The bottom radio button gives you the power to restore a specific file from the Windows 98 CD-ROM installation disc, provided of course that you know the exact name of the file you want to restore.

10. To begin the scanning process, click once on the `Start` button.

> **NOTE**
>
> The two radio button options will immediately be grayed-out and the System File Checker utility will commence its examination of your computer's system files. Your system will become sluggish if you try to use any other applications at the same time that the System File Checker tool is active.

11. The System File Checker utility displays a Finished message. Click `OK` to close the utility.
12. Alternatively, click `Details...` to view the System File Checker Results window. This informational message box provides you with the details about what the utility did to your computer. After examining the data, click `OK` to close this window.
13. Click `OK` to close the Finished screen, and click `OK` again to exit out of the System File Checker utility completely.

> **WARNING**
>
> The System SFC was designed with IT professionals in mind. Unless a system configuration file is logged immediately after the Windows 98 installation (BEFORE any users apps are installed), the System File Checker will not be able to restore a true default configuration and might not restore damaged files with the correct defaults.

SYSTEM INFORMATION

The System Information utility for Windows 98 does exactly as its name implies: It provides you with information about your computer system and software. It also serves as the launching point for several effective system utilities. By incorporating all this information together, the user can troubleshoot almost any problem from this one utility.

Use System Information

1. Click once on the [Start] button, then choose **Programs, Accessories, System Tools, System Information**. The Microsoft System Information screen opens.
2. Click once on the plus (+) symbol next to any category in either pane to reveal even more data.
3. Click once on any option within a specific category to reveal detailed information about that topic.
4. Click once on the **Tools** menu to access several other Windows 98 utilities:
    - The Update Wizard Uninstall Tool
    - The Signature Verification Tool
    - The System File Checker
    - The Registry Checker
    - The Automatic Skip Driver Agent
    - Dr. Watson
    - The System Configuration Utility
    - ScanDisk
    - The Version Conflict Manager

> **NOTE**
> Although these tools will most certainly aid any information systems (IS) professional, they will probably cause information overload for the basic Windows 98 user.

5. To save your system information data to a separate file, click on **File, Export**. This opens the Save As window where you can navigate to the folder where you want the file to be saved.
6. In the Save As window, type a name for the file you are exporting (it will be saved in a text format), and then click once on the **Save** option. Even on fast computer systems, this process takes several minutes to complete.

See Also Registry, ScanDisk, System File Checker

TASKBAR PROPERTIES

The Windows 98 taskbar is the long, rectangular box that contains the [Start] button, **Clock**, **System Tray**, and **Quick Launch** icons. Whenever a Windows application or folder is running, a button representing that application also appears in the taskbar. Although the taskbar appears along the bottom of the desktop by default, it can be moved to either side or to the top of your screen.

The Windows 98 taskbar serves many purposes, including providing easy access to applications and folders as well as to the Internet. New to Windows 98 is the capability for users to create as many new taskbars as they want (it is not a great idea to create too many, but this is a nice feature nonetheless).

Configure Your Taskbar

1. Right-click on an empty area of the taskbar and choose **Properties** from the menu that appears.
2. The **Taskbar Options** tab of the Taskbar Properties window appears. You can modify the appearance of your taskbar by checking any of the following items:
    - **Always on Top**—This option will determine whether your taskbar remains on your desktop or gets placed on top of any active folders or applications.
    - **Auto Hide**—This option allows you to place your taskbar just off your desktop. To view a hidden taskbar, simply move your mouse pointer all the way to the edge of the desktop where your taskbar usually lies. It will automatically appear.
    - **Show Small Icons in Start Menu**—This option allows your monitor to display smaller than normal icons on the taskbar.
    - **Show Clock**—This option will place a small clock on the right side of your toolbar.
3. Click once on the **Start Menu Programs** tab to view the next screen. Here you can add items to or remove

items from your **Start** menu, as well as clear the contents of the Documents menu.

4. To add an item to the **Start** menu, click once on the `Add...` button. This starts the **Create Shortcut** Wizard.

5. If you know the full path for the shortcut you want to add, type it in the **Command line** text field. If not, click `Browse...` to open the **Browse** window.

6. Navigate to the folder that contains the file for the shortcut you want to add. Click once on the file, and then click once on the `Open` button to continue. Notice that the path and filename are automatically entered in the **Command line** field.

7. Click once on the `Next >` button to continue to the Select Program Folder screen. If you want to create a new area in your **Start** menu for the shortcut you want to add, click once on the `New Folder...` button. Otherwise, simply locate the folder in which you want to house the shortcut, and then click once on the `Next >` button to continue.

8. In the Select a Title for the Program screen, type a descriptive name for your shortcut (this is the name that will appear in the **Start** menu).

9. Click once on the `Finish` button to complete this process. Your newly created shortcut is now part of the **Start Menu** structure.

Add a New Toolbar to the Taskbar

1. Right-click on a blank area of the taskbar, click once on the **Toolbars** menu option, and then choose the **New Toolbar** selection.

2. In the **New Toolbar** window, type the location on the hard drive where the new toolbar should point. Click one of the folders or type an Internet address (such as http://www.microsoft.com/siteserver/), and then click once on the `OK` button. Your newly created toolbar appears on the Windows 98 taskbar.

> **TIP**
> You can easily modify the location of the taskbar and alter the way it appears on the desktop. To move the taskbar to right, left, right, or bottom of your desktop, simply click on the taskbar and drag and drop the taskbar to the location you want.

See Also Documents Menu, Start Menu, Toolbars

TCP/IP

Transmission Control Protocol/Internet Protocol (TCP/IP) is the networking protocol (or language) that forms the basis of the Internet. This language is how computers and networks communicate with each other. One of the nicest things about TCP/IP is that for the most part it all happens behind the scenes.

When you connect to the Internet (or to your company's intranet/extranet), the Web server or network administrator will assign an address to your PC. This address lets the server know how to route the information you want to see to your desktop. IP addresses consist of a series of four octets (or 32-bits). Thus, an address within your firm might be something like this: 130.130.10.57. Each octet, within your IP address, can contain any number between 1–254.

> **WARNING**
> Unless you are willing and interested in really reading up on the principles behind the TCP/IP technology, I strongly recommend that you let your Internet provider or network administrator talk you through any configuration necessary. One slight error here can cause major time and hassles to find and to correct.

TELEPHONY PROPERTIES

Telephony is the process by which your PC is able to communicate and send commands over the telephone system to other PC and telephone devices, such as modems, faxes, telephones, and so on. This feature also eliminates the need to close one modem-using application to start another. For example, say you have a program set up to receive a call, but want to place a fax in the mean time.

Configure Telephony Screens

1. Click once on the **Start** button, choose **Settings, Control Panel**.
2. Double-click the **Telephony** icon in the Control Panel window.
3. Click once on the **Telephony Drivers** tab in the Dialing Properties window to view that screen.

> **NOTE**
> When hardware devices such as ISDN modems and the like are first installed, their drivers automatically show up in this screen. Therefore, it is unlikely that you will ever use the **Add** button to install new telephony drivers into your Windows 98 system.

4. To remove a driver, click once on the driver you want to remove to select it, and then click once on the **Remove** button.
5. To configure a particular driver, click once on that driver to select it, and click once on the **Configure** button. Then follow the prompts to complete the process.
6. Click once on the **OK** button to accept any changes and exit the Dialing Properties dialog.

See Also Comic Chat, Dial-Up Networking, HyperTerminal, ISDN Configuration Wizard, Modem Properties, NetMeeting, Outlook Express Email Client, Phone Dialer

TIME

Windows 98 keeps track of the system date and time for the computer. It is easy to view the time by just moving your mouse pointer over the Windows 98 taskbar so that the time display becomes visible.

Set the Time

1. Double-click the time display on the taskbar to open the Date/Time Properties screen. You will see a large clock, with a digital read-out of the current time just below it.
2. You can alter the time either by using the up/down arrows found on the side of that digital read-out area or by simply clicking on the current date to highlight it first and then typing in the correct time. You may also change the time from **AM** to **PM** (or vice versa) using this same procedure.
3. Click once on the OK button to force Windows 98 to accept your changes to the time, which will also close this Date/Time Properties screen.

See Also Date/Time, Taskbar

TOOLBARS

A toolbar, in Windows 98 terminology, is nothing more than a starting point for launching applications, programs, and/or utilities. There are a few standard toolbars found in the Windows 98 operating system:

- Address
- Channel Bar
- Desktop
- Links
- Quick Launch

The Address Toolbar

A good example of a toolbar is the Address toolbar. You will see this one throughout Windows 98 and its various applications, as this is the toolbar where you will actually type in an Internet address or a location on your computer. You might recognize this toolbar as an Internet Explorer user. Essentially, it looks just like a plain white box with an open area for typing, and will have the label Address directly to the left of the box. In addition, you can actually use the Address toolbar to replace the folders list in Windows Explorer and My Computer. Use toolbar to quickly jump to locations on your hard drive or the Internet.

See Also Internet Explorer

The Channel Bar

The Channel Bar contains links to multiple sites and topic groups on the World Wide Web. It is similar to your Favorites menu except that it is easier to subscribe to these sites and channel groups. Subscribing allows the sites, networks, and topics that you select to "push," or send directly to your PC, regular updates to the information that you decide you are interested in. Go to the "Channels" section in this book for information on how to modify this toolbar.

See Also Channels, Favorites, Internet Explorer

The Desktop Toolbar

The Desktop toolbar takes all the standard desktop icons (**My Computer**, **Network Neighborhood**, **Recycle Bin**, **Internet Explorer**, and **My Briefcase**) along with any other shortcuts or folders that you might have added to your desktop, and automatically drops a copy of them onto a toolbar for you.

> **NOTE**
> Anytime you add, delete, or rename a shortcut on your desktop; your Desktop toolbar will be automatically updated to match.

See Also Active Desktop

The Link Toolbar

A Link toolbar is just like a shortened Favorites menu on the Windows 98 Start Menu. This toolbar provides you with shortcuts or "links" directly to Internet/intranet/extranet sites (usually Web or HTML-based sites), which having been chosen by Microsoft because they serve as information gateways. And, just like the Favorites menu, simply clicking on the buttons will take you to where you want to go.

To modify your Links toolbar, follow these steps:

1. To alter the destination Web site for a specific button, right-click on it to bring up the shortcut menu.
2. Choose **Properties**, and then the **Internet Shortcut** tab. From here, you can change the URL to the one you want.
3. If you want to change the order of the buttons on your Links menu, you can just drag them to where you want with your mouse.
4. To add new Links buttons to your toolbar, all you have to do is click on a hyperlink and drag it to a spot on your Links toolbar.
5. To change the display attributes of your toolbar, choose **Start**, **Favorites**, **Organize Favorites**, **Links**. There you can delete, rename, and move the buttons on your Links toolbar.

See Also Favorites Menu, Internet Explorer

The Quick Launch Toolbar

The Quick Launch toolbar contains shortcuts that permit you to jump to another program, application, physical disk location, or to the Internet without going through the standard set of Windows 98 menu options (that is, **Start**, **Programs**, and so on). When Windows 98 is installed, it will automatically create the Quick Launch toolbar and place into the left side of your Windows 98 taskbar (just to the right of the **Start** button). The four default shortcuts are: Launch Internet Explorer Browser, Launch Outlook Express, Show Desktop, and View Channels.

To add or delete shortcuts from this toolbar, follow these steps:

1. Choose **Start**, **Programs**, **Windows Explorer** to open the Windows Explorer window.

2. Locate the program that you would like to add by browsing through the folders in the left window pane.
3. Right-click on the application file to select it and to bring up the shortcut menu; select Copy.
4. Find and select the folder:

   ```
   C:\Windows\Application Data\Microsoft\Internet Explorer\QuickLaunch
   ```

   If your computer has multiple users, you might need to look for the following:

   ```
   C:\Windows\Profiles\user name\Application Data\Microsoft\Internet Explorer\QuickLaunch
   ```

5. Press Ctrl+V to paste a shortcut of the file into the Quick Launch folder.
6. Remove any unwanted shortcuts by clicking once on the shortcut, and then pressing the Del key on your keyboard. Click Yes to send the shortcut to the Recycle Bin, and click No if you've changed your mind.
7. Click the × button in the upper-right corner to close Windows Explorer. Expect to restart your computer before you see your new icon in the Quick Launch toolbar.

See Also Active Desktop, Channels, Internet Explorer, Outlook Express

UNINSTALL WINDOWS 98

To uninstall the Windows 98 operating system, you must have used the **Save Previous Version** option when you conducted the Windows 98 installation process, in which case the uninstall process is not too difficult. If your PC came with Windows 98 preinstalled, then this feature is probably not available to you. Also, if you have since upgraded your PC from the FAT16 file system to FAT32, then the uninstall option will not be available as it is removed during the FAT32 conversion routine.

Uninstall Windows 98

1. Click once on the [Start] button, then choose **Settings, Control Panel**.
2. Double-click the **Add/Remove Programs** icon in the **Control Panel** window to access the **Add/Remove Programs Properties** screen.
3. Scroll towards the bottom until you see the **Uninstall Windows 98** listing. Click once on that listing to select it, and then click once on the [ ] button.
4. Follow the prompts and restart your computer when prompted.

> **NOTE**
>
> If you installed any Windows 98-specific applications, such as the Windows 98 Resource Kit, you will no longer be able to use those software applications. You must reinstall the Windows 95 or Windows 3.x versions (depending on which operating system was on your PC before your upgrade to Windows 98) of those applications for you to use them in the future.

See Also Add/Remove Programs

UPGRADE WINDOWS 98

You can install Windows 98 directly over a previous version of Microsoft Windows (either Windows 3.1 or Windows 95), thereby upgrading your system.

> **NOTE**
>
> Computers containing Windows versions 3.0, 386, 286, and 1.0 must be upgraded to Windows 3.1 before Windows 98 can be installed on them. However, it is extremely unlikely (and for the 1.0 and 286 versions, probably technically impossible) that any of the PCs that were designed to run these earlier versions of Windows could have their hardware upgraded enough to support even the most basic installation of Windows 95, much less Windows 98!

See Also Install Windows 98 Directly from a CD-ROM Disc

USER PROFILES

User profiles in Windows 98 enable multiple users to operate the same PC. Each user will have his or her own personalized desktop with specific settings, screen savers, backgrounds, and so forth.

Configure User Profiles

1. Click once on the [Start] button, choose **Settings, Control Panel**.
2. Double-click the **Users** icon in the **Control Panel** window. The **Enable Multi-User Settings** Wizard will then start.
3. If you are the main user, type your name in the wizard's **Add User** screen. If you are not the main user of this computer, you should type in the name of the person who is the primary user of this PC. Click once on the [Next>] button to continue.
4. If you want to use a password, type it in the **Password** field of the **Enter New Password** screen. Confirm the password by typing it again in the **Confirm** password field, and then click once on the [Next>] button to continue.

> **NOTE**
>
> If you do not want to require a password, then simply leave both boxes blank.

> **NOTE**
> Unfortunately, a Windows 98 password does not really protect a PC. Instead, it just slows the person who is accessing your data down a bit (pressing the Esc key on the keyboard will bypass the password screen prompt).

5. In the **Personalized Items Settings** screen, click the items you want to personalize, and then specify whether you want to create copies of current items and their content or to create new items to save disk space.

> **NOTE**
> It is recommended that you create copies if this is a home PC, and create new items if this computer is used in a corporate or professional work environment. The reason for this is simple enough: On a home PC you will probably want every user to see all the same installed applications and desktop/Start menu icons, whereas in a business environment each user will probably have specific tasks that are not necessarily the same (if they are, then you probably will want to create copies for them as well).

6. Click once on the **Next >** button to continue.
7. Click once on the **Finish** button in the final screen to complete the wizard.
8. You will see a message status box while the new user's profile is being created. After the profile is created, you are prompted to restart your computer. Click once on the **Yes** button so the new user account can be used.

An Alternative Way to Configure User Profiles

1. Double-click the **Passwords** icon in the **Control Panel** window.
2. Click once on the **User Profiles** tab in the **Passwords Properties** window to access the next screen.

3. Click once on the second radio button to enable users to customize their preferences and desktop settings. This enables the **User** profile settings section in the lower half of the tab.
4. If you want a completely custom environment, check the second check box so that the **Start** menu and **Program** groups are included in the user settings. Otherwise, leave the top box checked so that the desktop icons are set to specific users.
5. Restart the computer to effect these changes.

VIRTUAL PRIVATE NETWORKING

Virtual Private Networking (VPN) is a networking structure that provides a secure connection between two sites across either public networks (such as the Internet) or private networks. VPN relies upon a new networking protocol known as a *tunneling protocol*; the Windows 98 version of VPN uses PPTP (Point-to-Point Tunneling Protocol).

PPTP comes in handy should you be trying to connect to your company's computer systems, but your method of transport is the public Internet. In this case, you would probably want to keep your information as private as possible. The Windows 98 VPN with PPTP allows just this. It gives you sort of your own encrypted "tunnel" that goes directly through the Internet, and automatically prevents others from "looking" into your tunnel of information.

Configure a Virtual Private Network Connection

1. Click once on the [Start] button, then choose **Settings**, **Control Panel**.

2. Double-click the **Network** icon in the **Control Panel** window to access the **Network Properties** screen.

3. In the **Configuration** tab of the Network screen, scroll through the components list to determine whether a VPN adapter, such as the Microsoft Virtual Private Network Adapter (which is the software driver required to run a VPN connection), is installed.

4. If you fail to find an adapter, click once on the [Add] button to begin installing one. This opens the **Select Network Component Type** screen. Click once on the **Adapter** option, and then click once on the [OK] button.

5. The **Select Network Adapters** window appears. If you have an installation disk from the manufacturer of your VPN device, click once on the [Have Disk...] button and follow the prompts. Otherwise, click once on the name of your VPN device's manufacturer in the left pane, and then click once on the name of your VPN device in the

right side pane. Click once on the [OK] button to continue.

6. You are returned to the Network dialog. You will see the Microsoft Virtual Private Networking device appears in the network component list. Click once on the [OK] button to accept this change, and follow the prompts for installing the appropriate software drivers for the VPN device.

> **NOTE**
>
> Keep in mind that your organization will need to configure its server/host side of the VPN equation, in order for you to make a secure connection between your Windows 98 PC and the server/host computer system(s).

See Also Dial-Up Networking

VOLUME CONTROL

The Volume Control feature of the Windows 98 operating system does exactly what you probably expect: It controls the volume settings for your multimedia devices such as the CD Player, sound card speakers, TV tuner, and so on.

Use Volume Control

1. Click once on the [Start] button, choose **Programs**, **Accessories**, **Entertainment**, and then select **Volume Control**.

2. The **Volume Control** screen appears. Use the slider bars to control the volume output for each of the devices shown on the screen. Clicking the [Advanced...] button in the **Microphone Balance** section will offer a few additional options (not all PCs have this button).

3. After you make your changes, exit the screen by clicking the × button in the upper-right corner of the screen.

WAVETOP DATA BROADCASTING

WaveTop Data Broadcasting is a new wireless technology that allows you to acquire the "Best of the Web" content, as well as software downloads, without using either an ISP or a telephone line. This almost sounds like a little bit of magic, doesn't it? Well, it is close. WaveTop uses a combination of your local television service and the TV Tuner card installed in your PC.

> **NOTE**
>
> If you do not own a TV Tuner card, then this service (just like WebTV) is not for you. Likewise, this technology is not quite ready for laptop/notebook prime time, so to speak. So, do not attempt to use it without first possessing a solid knowledge of your computer's hardware and internal components.

Install WaveTop Data Broadcasting

1. To install the WaveTop Data Broadcasting service you need to use the Add/Remove Programs feature of the Windows 98 operating system. This service is found inside the **Web TV for Windows** selection box. You will need to click once on the [Details] button to see the actual **WaveTop Data Broadcasting** service option.

2. You must restart Windows 98 to start the **WaveTop Data Broadcasting** service. Click once on the [Start] button, then choose **Programs**, **Accessories**, and **WaveTop**.

3. The **WaveTop Network Initialization** window appears. This portion of the configuration process takes roughly 10 minutes to complete.

> **NOTE**
>
> The WaveTop software will continue its configuration process by scanning all the TV channels in your viewing area in an attempt to find the local PBS (public broadcasting station) station. During this process, the WaveTop Receiver Channel Scan window will automatically appear.
>
> This screen does a nice job of estimating the time remaining for the scanning process. If you receive an error message stating that a compatible WaveTop channel could not be found, keep trying. It works on a sporadic basis, even in the largest metropolitan areas in the United States.

See Also Add/Remove Programs, WebTV for Windows

WEB PUBLISHING WIZARD

The Windows 98 Web Publishing Wizard provides an easy way to place, or *publish*, your Web pages or sites on an Internet or intranet hosting service.

Use the Web Publishing Wizard

1. Click the **Start** button, then choose **Programs**, **Internet Explorer**, **Web Publishing Wizard**.
2. The Publish Your Files on the Web screen of the Web Publishing Wizard provides information about the wizard. Click **Next >** to continue.
3. Select the file or folder that you want to publish to the Web. If you do not know the entire path to the folder or file, either click once on the **Browse Folders...** button or the **Browse Files...** button. After the file or folder name is selected, click **Next >** to continue.
4. In the Name the Web Server screen, type a descriptive name for your Web server. If you know the connection method for your Web-hosting service or LAN, click once on the **Advanced...** button to continue to the Select Your Connection Method screen. If you are unsure, click **Next >** to let the Web Publishing Wizard attempt to make this setting automatically.
5. Specify the appropriate Connection Method from the drop-down list, and then click **Next >** to continue.

> **NOTE**
>
> It is very important that you select the correct connection method; failure to do so might result in your page being shown either incorrectly or not at all. When in doubt, either skip this advanced screen or select the **Automatically Select Service Provider** option. This might alleviate some potential trouble down the road.

6. Specify the URL needed to access your Web pages and the local directory location of your Web files on your hard drive, and then click [Next>] to continue.

> **NOTE**
>
> The URL (Uniform Resource Locator) is used to locate the Internet or intranet site, while the local directory is used to locate files on your hard drive.

7. If your Web hosting service or network requires a password, you will see the Enter Network Password screen. Enter your **User Name** and **Password**, and click [OK]. After you have entered your password and/or you do not need to provide one, you will be taken to the Provide Posting Information dialog.

> **NOTE**
>
> If the **Enter Network Password** dialog appears and your Web hosting service or LAN does not require a password, don't panic. It could be one of two things. Either, you selected the wrong **Connection Method** or the Web Publishing Wizard selected the wrong method for you. Just click [Cancel] and then [Next>] to skip to the **Select Your Connection Method** screen.
>
> If you asked the wizard to select your connection method and it was unable to, you will see the **Specify a Connection Method** screen. Click [Next>] to get to the **Select Your Connection Method** screen.
>
> Manually select the appropriate **Connection Method** from the drop-down list and click [Next>]. (If you don't know what the right choice is, check with your Web hosting service or system administrator.)

8. Enter the **Server name, Posting Command, Use SSL (Secure Sockets Layer), Post-processing Required**, and its associated **URL** as required by your Web hosting service.

> **NOTE**
>
> The **Provide Posting Information** dialog box gathers the specific information required by your Web hosting service and/or your intranet server. Without the correct information here, your Web server will not be able to post your Web page to the proper place and with the correct protocols.
>
> All the information required in this screen should be obtained from your network system administrator (if you are posting to your company's intranet site) or your Web hosting service (if you are posting to an Internet site).

9. After you have made your selections, click [Next >] to be taken to the Publish Your Files screen. Click once on the [Finish] button to publish your files and to close the wizard. You should now be able to view the site online.

See Also Front Page Express

WEBTV FOR WINDOWS

WebTV for Windows enables your PC to display both standard and interactive television broadcasts, to access regular Internet content, as well as to view a personalized online Interactive Program Guide.

You already know what standard television broadcasts are; you watch it every day on television. But, did you know that several shows also have a whole range of interactive features available through the World Wide Web. With WebTV, you can watch the show, chat with other watchers, look up background information about the stars and plots, and play games and trivia all at the same time. You can receive both standard and interactive TV broadcasts only if you have a TV Tuner card (a hardware device for receiving television broadcasts) installed on your PC.

WebTV can also use your TV Tuner card to pick up Internet broadcast signals in the same way that it picks up your local television programming, via airwaves. What this means is that you can download Web sites and files to your PC, and view them all without ever using your telephone line.

In addition, you can use WebTV even if you don't have a TV Tuner card. Using your zip code and your cable provider, WebTV can provide you with a personalized Interactive Program Guide. In addition to scrolling through your guide, you can also search it by show, star, subject, and type.

Use **Add/Remove Programs** to install the WebTV for Windows, if it is not already present on your computer.

Use WebTV for Windows

1. Click once on the [Start] button, then choose **Programs**, **Accessories**, **Entertainment**, and then **WebTV for Windows**.
2. The WebTV introductory screen appears. Your system will pause here for a few seconds before taking you directly to the **WebTV Program Guide** screen. Scroll up and down this screen to figure out what television shows are scheduled in your area.

> **NOTE**
> As part of the installation process for WebTV, you will be prompted for your zip code. This is how the software knows where you live.

3. Click once on the **Search** tab to view that screen. Type in the text string that you want to search for, and then click on the [SEARCH] button to initiate the search. Once you have found the show that you are seeking, click on it once to highlight it and then click on the watch button (on the right side of the screen).

> **NOTE**
>
> The far-left portion of the **Search** tab features a scrollable **Categories** list. The television shows are split into areas such as Action or Drama by the WebTV service automatically. At present, you can't modify this organizational feature.
>
> Think of the **Categories** listing as a quick way to find a TV show that you want to watch, but are not really sure what the name of it is. The way you use this listing is similar to "channel surfing" without actually using your TV remote.

4. To reconfigure your WebTV settings, you must first return to the channel guide, so click once on the **Guide** tab to move to that screen.

5. Double-click **Channel 96** on the dial to access the **Configuration** area.

6. If you want to take the interactive multimedia tour, click once on the [Next>] button at the bottom of the screen, and off you go!

7. Otherwise, move your mouse pointer up to the top of the screen to "pull down" the menu. From there, you should click on the [Settings...] button to adjust your settings.

8. In the configuration area, you can choose to "block" channels (by de-selecting them) for parental control. You can also add closed captioning to your screen (this is helpful for the hard of hearing or if you have poor computer speakers). Click [OK] to go back the Program Guide.

See Also Add/Remove Programs, WaveTop Data Broadcasting

WELCOME TO WINDOWS

The Windows 98 Welcome to Windows screen will automatically appear the first time you start your computer after installing Windows 98. If you want the screen to continue to appear at start up time, check the check box in the bottom-left corner of the screen.

Access the Welcome to Windows Screen

1. Click once on the [Start] button, then choose **Programs, System Tools, Welcome to Windows**.
2. The **Welcome to Windows 98** screen appears. Click any of the options in the **Contents** menu to jump directly to that online topic. Alternatively, you can position your mouse pointer over one of these options to view information about it on the right portion of the screen.

> **NOTE**
>
> The **Welcome to Windows 98** screen initially shown to you will vary slightly from the one that you see after you register your copy of Windows 98. The first time you see this screen the **Register Windows 98** option will be present. However, once you register your copy of Windows 98, the top option will disappear from this screen, and you will not see it again at any point in the future. This is normal, so do not be alarmed.

WINDOWS EXPLORER

Windows Explorer is the most important end-user application in Windows 98. All of the data present on your computer is displayed as drives, folders, subfolders, files, and so on. You can view, add, copy, move, rename, and delete both files and folders with Windows Explorer. You will soon realize that is used inside most Windows applications, behind [Browse...] buttons, as the basis for the **Find, Open**, and **Save** commands, and as a core component of the Internet Explorer Web browser.

> **NOTE**
>
> If you have recently upgraded to Windows 98 from Windows 3.0 or 3.1x, then just think of **Windows Explorer** as the replacement to the utility you knew as **File Manager**.

Use Windows Explorer

1. Click once on the [Start] button, then choose **Programs, Windows Explorer**.

2. The main **Windows Explorer** screen appears. The contents of this screen represent the contents of your computer. Using the scrollbar, scroll down the left pane until you find the drive letter that represents your hard drive (probably the letter **C**).

3. Click the drive letter; and the contents of that drive automatically appear in the right pane.

4. That is all you need to do. You are now an expert at using the **Windows Explorer** tool.

See Also My Computer

WINDOWS MEDIA PLAYER

The Windows Media Player enables you to play a wide assortment of multimedia file types including ActiveMovie, Mpact MPEG Decoder, Video for Windows, Sound (WAV), MIDI Sequencer, MP3, and CD Audio files. (You might even be able to play a few additional types, depending upon your computer's sound equipment.)

Use Media Player

1. Click once on the [Start] button, then choose **Programs, Accessories, Entertainment,** and **Windows Media Player**. The primary **Windows Media Player** window appears.

2. To select a media file for playing, select **File, Open**. The **Open** dialog appears.

3. Navigate to the folder that contains the file you want to view. Select the file by clicking on it once, and then click once on the [Open] button. You will then be returned to the main Media Player window with the file that you selected ready to be played.

4. Click once on the [▶] button (the one on the far left that resembles a single right arrow). When the music starts, the marker on the time line moves to show how much time has elapsed and how much is remaining.

> **NOTE**
> Had you selected a file that contained video (such as MPEG, some AVI files, and the like), you would then also see that image appear in the middle of the **Windows Media Player** screen.

See Also Multimedia Properties

WINDOWS 98 RESOURCE KIT

Microsoft created a CD, commonly known as the Windows 98 Resource Kit, chock full of tools and utilities that pertain to the Windows 98 operating system. Along with it they include a brief 1,900+–page book to explain how to use all those tools with the Windows 98 operating system. These tools and utilities make it much easier to deploy, troubleshoot, support, administer, and manage Windows 98. Additionally, the Resource Kit provides specific tools that aid in the Windows 98 scripting process, make it much more palatable to edit and manipulate the registry, and permit you to compare files much quicker and easier. There is a catch, of course; the Windows 98 Resource Kit CD-ROM comes with its nearly 2,000 page Resource Kit book and will set you back $69.99 (USD). If you aren't sure whether the kit would be worth the price, you can review the Resource Sampler Kit that comes with your Windows 98 CD and decide for yourself.

Networking or desktop systems professionals benefit the most from the Windows 98 Resource Kit because they are required to support large numbers of Windows 98 computers. Help Desk professionals who support countless numbers of Windows 98 users, will also benefit from the Resource Kit. The book accompanying the Resource Kit does not have pictures, and it does not have a systematic format, and does not express itself well to the entry-level technical person, not to mention non-technical layperson. Its audience is really aimed at the technically perceptive, power users of Windows 98. The Resource Kit tools on the accompanying CD-ROM are also not documented well.

Therefore, if you are an entry-level user of Windows 98 you might find that many of these tools are too advanced for you. Many of these tools require you to be able to figure things out on your own, so you should be prepared to do so (or continue reading this book for more assistance).

WINDOWS 98 SECOND EDITION

Microsoft Corporation is presently in the midst of creating an update release to its original Windows 98 operating system (first released on 25 June 1998). This new release, which goes above and beyond those additional utilities, tools, and freebies that are presently available on the Windows 98 Windows Update Internet Web site. You might want to think of this new release as a major Service Pack update patch (a file that Microsoft provides to fix bugs, update, and/or enhance applications) to the operating system. However, this update has one major difference: this patch is so integrated into the Windows 98 operating system that it had to be released as an entirely different version. Hence, the new name: Windows 98 Second Edition.

WINDOWS UPDATE

Quite frequently, Microsoft will post updates to its Windows 98 operating system to its Internet Web site. Individual Windows 98 users, as well as corporate system administrators responsible for thousands of computers will want at least some of these updates. The process for getting these updates is easy. All it requires is a connection to the Internet, either dial-up or a direct connection (the high-speed connection is preferred, obviously), and the use of an Internet Web browser (the version of Microsoft's Internet Explorer that is integrated into the Windows 98 OS is preferred, but Netscape might work somewhat okay as well).

In addition to periodic manual updates, Microsoft now has a utility patch that you can install on your PC that will notify you when you connect to the Internet if a patch is available. This utility is called Critical Update Notification.

Update Your Windows 98 Software

1. Connect to the Internet via a Dial-Up Networking connection or a LAN/WAN direct connection.
2. To access the initial **Microsoft Windows Update** Web site, either click [Start], **Windows Update**.

> **NOTE**
>
> When you connect to this site for the first time, ActiveX control will install on your computer. You will notice a series of tabs along the left side of the window (**Windows Update Home Page**, **Product Updates**, and **Member Services**). These tabs control access to the entire site, and they can be used to quickly jump to another location on the Web site. For example, if you have moved and need to update your physical (your home) or logical (email) address with Microsoft, then you would click the **Member Services** tab; this causes the tab to expand with other selections.

3. Click once on the **Product Updates** tab, located on the main Windows Update Web site. It might take a few seconds for the **Product Catalog** page to initialize. Eventually the **Windows Update** message box will appear.
4. It is strongly recommended that you reply [Yes] when asked, "**Would you like to check now?**" This will permit a more accurate updating of your Windows 98 PC. However, if you are hoping to access an update for use with many computers, you might want to click [No] and skip this step.
5. Microsoft displays a list of available components and updates for your computer. If you scroll down through the list, you see that they have selected the components that are either absent from your computer or that are updates to the applications you already have. You can go through this list and check additional items or uncheck some of theirs as you see fit.

6. Scroll down to the bottom of the screen after you have finished making all of your choices. The Microsoft Windows Update Web site automatically presents an estimated download time for you, based on the selected components.

7. Click once on the [Download] button to initiate the download process after you are satisfied with all of the options presented.

8. Again, Microsoft attempts to confirm your choices. If they are correct, click once on the [Start Download] button to initiate the download process.

9. Be patient. This process goes very slow at times. If you can't wait any longer, you can click once on the [Cancel] button to terminate the download. This will permit you to try a smaller download instead or nothing at all.

10. **Microsoft Update** will automatically apply the downloaded patches to your system. Click once on the [OK] button to confirm the download process.

11. If prompted, shut down all open applications and restart your computer to complete the installation process.

Use Critical Update Notification

1. Connect to the Internet via a Dial-Up Networking connection or a LAN/WAN direct connection.

2. To access the initial **Microsoft Windows Update** Web site, either click [Start], **Windows Update**.

3. Click once on the **Product Updates** tab, and wait for the **Product Catalog** page to initialize.

4. It is strongly recommended that you reply [Yes] when asked, "**Would you like to check now?**"

5. Scroll down through the list of available components and updates for your computer and look for **Windows Critical Update Notification**. If you want more information about this update, click **Read This First**.

6. Check the box next to the **Windows Critical Update Notification** list item, and click [Download] to continue.

7. Again, Microsoft attempts to confirm your choices. If they are correct, click once on the [Start Download] button to initiate the download process.

> **NOTE**
> After you download this patch, any time you access the Internet and a new critical update is available for your system, you will be notified and given the opportunity to download it.

8. Microsoft Update will automatically apply the downloaded patches to your system. Click once on the [OK] button to confirm the download process.
9. If prompted, shut down all open applications and restart your computer to complete the installation process.

WINPOPUP

WinPopup provides a great way to send electronic messages between two or more users over a LAN (local area network).

Use WinPopup

1. Click once on the [Start] button and then choose the **Run** option.
2. In the **Run** dialog, type the command: WinPopup and then click once on the [OK] button to continue.
3. Click once on the [envelope] button in the **WinPopup** window to initiate a message send.
4. Type the name (system logon ID) of the computer, user, or workgroup that you want to receive the message, and then type the message in the box below. Click once on the [OK] button to transmit the message.
5. You are returned to the main **WinPopup** screen. Click once on the [Options..] button to view the next screen, where you can check any or all of the three options. Click once on the [OK] button to accept all the changes.

6. You will then be returned to the main **WinPopup** screen. When you close **WinPopup**, a warning message box might appear, which is informational in nature only. Click once on the [OK] button to end the session.

WORDPAD

WordPad is a small word processing program, which is built into Windows 98. Like Notepad, a built-in Microsoft text editor, WordPad enables you to create and edit text. However, WordPad also gives you the ability to format your text to improve its appearance.

Use WordPad

1. Click once on the [Start] button, then choose **Programs**, **Accessories**, and **WordPad**.
2. The **WordPad** window will appear. To begin using the application, just start typing in the whitespace as soon as the program begins.
3. You can create a new file by choosing **File, New**.
4. To edit an existing file you must first open it by clicking on **File**, and then on **Open**. You will see a window appear, which permits you to navigate to the file that you want to open. Click once on that file to select it, and then click once on the [Open] button to continue.

> **NOTE**
> The **Files of type** drop-down box lists the file types supported by WordPad.

5. The file you just selected opens onto the desktop. Make your changes, and then click once on the **File** menu option and then choose **Save**, **Print**, or **Exit**.

See Also NotePad

WORKGROUP NAME

Like most of the other networking configurations that need to be performed in the Windows 98 operating system, the system identification parameters also need to be set. The Workgroup name identifies the group of computers that you most often connect to and work with.

Set Your Workgroup Name

1. Click [Start], **Settings**, **Control Panel** to open that window.

2. Double-click the **Network** icon to reveal the **Network** dialog.

> **TIP**
>
> Alternatively, if you already have at least one network software client installed, you can quickly access the Network screen pressing the [Alt] key on your keyboard while double-clicking the **Network Neighborhood** icon found on the Windows 98 Desktop.

3. When the **Network** screen appears, move to the **Identification** tab by clicking on it once.

4. Enter the name of the Workgroup. If you share information and resources with others, list the name of that group as your Workgroup Name. The name cannot exceed 15 characters (numbers and letters are acceptable). Click [OK] to save your changes and exit the Network dialog.

> **NOTE**
>
> It is very important that you do not attempt to set the Computer Name and the Workgroup Name as the same. Windows 98 does not permit these two fields to contain the same name.

5. Click once on the [Yes] button to permit Windows 98 to restart your computer system. The new Workgroup Name will take effect after the restart.

X-WINDOWS

X-Windows is a software term that actually applies to a graphical user interface (GUI) for a client workstation that either runs on some form of UNIX (an older, multitasking, text-based operating system typically found in academia or scientific communities) or by connecting to a UNIX file server. X-Windows has nothing to do with any form of Microsoft Windows, because Microsoft has never produced any X-Windows software.

x86

The moniker x86 is actually a shortened version of the term 80x86, where the *x* equates to a number. This number relates directly to the code number for an Intel Corporation central processing unit (CPU). For example, one of the early popular personal computers used an Intel processor known as an 80286 CPU, or "286" for short. So now whenever you see the term x86, you can automatically recognize that computer as having an Intel processor, which probably is running some version of Microsoft Windows: either Windows 98 or Windows NT Server/Workstation. Intel's trademarked term *Pentium* refers to what otherwise would have been the 80586 computer chip. Now we have the Pentium II (80686) and the Pentium III (80786) computer chips, which would have been named the 686 and 786 chips had Intel continued its original naming conventions.

YEAR 2000 (Y2K)

The year 2000 is just about upon us now. The gist of the Y2K issue is simple. In the heady days of mainframe computing as well as the early days of PC computing, software developers and the business managers who controlled the purse-strings were not foresighted enough to understand that saving two bytes of hard drive space for every year entered into their systems would ultimately cost them billions of dollars. This 2-byte savings for each of the millions or billions of date and time fields used back then is now resulting in the re-coding of all those original fields into century-compliant date and time fields. This money has been lost in both productivity as well as sheer development efforts, which have been focused on bringing these old or "legacy" systems applications and hardware up to date so that they can handle a four-digit year such as the year 2000.

Microsoft has been spending an incredible amount of time and money to ensure that all its current operating systems and software applications are up to date, including Windows 98. Of course, Windows 98 was not entirely Year 2000 compliant because Microsoft had to issue a special software patch. To obtain the patch or more details, access the site via this URL: http://www.microsoft.com/windows98/highlights/Win98Y2K.asp). Windows 98 can handle a system date of any year from 1980 up to the year 2099. Hopefully, this problem will not repeat itself 100 years from now.

ZERO ADMINISTRATION INITIATIVE (ZAIW)

Microsoft's recent foray into the world of network management and of lowering the total cost of ownership for an organization's deployment of Windows 98 technologies, has led it to launch an initiative known as the Zero Administration Initiative for Windows (ZAIW). This initiative actually comprises several software tools including the following:

- Internet Explorer Administration Kit's Profile Manager
- Windows Management Instrumentation (WMI)—The purpose of the WMI is to provide a basis for instrumentation in future Windows environments (READ: Windows 2000 Professional, Server, Advanced Server, and DataCenter, as well as Windows 98 Second Edition). This means that the WMI is just getting ready for prime time, especially in the Windows 98 world. However, it does include a set of extensions to the Win32 Driver Model (WDM), which will help to provide "hooks" to the future (and maybe even later use of Windows 98) operating systems environments.
- Microsoft Management Console (MMC)—This is a part of the Windows 98 Resource Kit.
- Web-Based Enterprise Management (WBEM)
- Microsoft Systems Management Server (SMS)—A Windows NT BackOffice component that allows for the close management of desktop computers and network devices.

The core focus of ZAIW is to open the infrastructure of Windows 98 to the rest of the world (so to speak). This means organizations can better manage their Windows 98 PCs as well as begin the establishment of a management infrastructure for lowering the TCO (Total Cost of Ownership) for a Windows 98 client base (inside a Windows NT server base).

Microsoft has announced several other technologies, both hardware and software that goes along with ZAIW.

However, because they have not been "officially" released to the retail market, this section will not discuss them in any detail. (Besides, the majority of these technologies are still in the "vaporware" stage—that is, the idea exists, but the "rubber" never meets the "road.")

Profile Manager Utility

The *Profile Manager* utility, which comes as a part of the *Internet Explorer Administration Kit*, is excellent at making sure that each of your organization's users are all accessing the Internet in a similar manner. The benefit to you is that when a user contacts your internal Help Desk (or other support infrastructure) for assistance, everyone should be able to provide a quick and consistent answer to the problem at hand. What this means, is that Tech support calls should be shorter in length, problems can be more easily resolved, and (hopefully, anyway) the organization's end user community will become more satisfied with the Information Services departments that exist in their company.

Microsoft Systems Management Server Software

The Microsoft *Systems Management Server Software* of Windows NT networking products, is an excellent tool for managing your Windows 98 Desktop client computers. Systems Management Server (SMS) excels at the following:

- The capability to monitor client computers.
- The capability to take hardware and software inventories of those same PCs.
- It can perform mass deployments of software (such as Microsoft Office and Windows 98).
- It can assist corporate help desks with its "remote control" capabilities (a help desk staff person can literally take control of a Windows 98 user's PC and see exactly what that user has done to "fix" their environment so that it no longer works correctly).
- It has a nice capability for identifying and fixing Year 2000 issues.

Windows Management Instrumentation (WMI)

The *Windows Management Instrumentation* (WMI) came about in part because of the NetPC debates and initiatives, which stem from Sun Microsystems' and Oracle's attempts to develop a "Windows-less" computer terminal system that would help companies lower their total cost of ownership of their sprawling desktop computer environments. WMI is optimized for the Windows platform. When coupled with WBEM, WMI provides a instrumentation mechanism within the Windows 98 platform that provides backward compatibility with legacy management instrumentation technologies such as the Desktop Management Initiative (DMI). In theory, the WMI technology will really take off when Microsoft releases its Windows 2000 server-based technologies (Server, Advanced Server, and DataCenter).

Web-Based Enterprise Management (WBEM)

Web-Based Enterprise Management (WBEM) comes with the Windows 98 operating system and needs to be installed separately, because it does not install with the full installation of Windows 98 (probably because most people would never know what to do with it). WBEM is an industrywide initiative (launched in July 1996, which included the likes of Cisco, Microsoft, Compaq, Intel, BMC Software, 3Com, Bay Networks, Dell, Hewlett-Packard, Tivoli Systems, Sybase, Symantec, Zenith, Attachmate, and Platinum Technologies) that includes a number of standards designed to allow management of systems, networks, and users through the use of Internet technologies. It defines schemas and protocols and is open and extensible. The Desktop Management Task Force (DMTF) has now ratified parts of it as the Common Information Model (CIM).

Microsoft Management Console (MMC)

The *Microsoft Management Console* (MMC) feature does not come with the Windows 98 operating system, but is a part of the Microsoft Windows 98 Resource Kit. The purpose of the MMC is to provide a standard framework display for hosting administration tools, which are built as MMC Snap-Ins by Microsoft and other third-party software vendors. The MMC has the potential for being used from within an existing enterprise console or to launch enterprise consoles.

Unlike some of the other enterprise consoles on the market today, the MMC imposes no protocol dependencies or object repositories: these remain the responsibility of each Snap-In. By allowing administrators to create their own views, and by removing technology discipline boundaries, it is possible to create appropriate displays of network, systems, and user information. This, in turn, provides a single point of management that is integrated, comprehensive, and easy to use.

All of this might sound great, but again there is some vaporware present in this technology. Microsoft is working hard on the MMC as part of the Windows 2000 operating systems. They have released miniaturized versions of the MMC as part of other applications (IIS 4.0, the Windows 98 Resource Kit, Site Server 3.0, for example), and it is clearly a "real" technology that the whole world can see and use on a stable, daily basis.

See Also Windows 98 Resource Kit

ZIPPED FILES (FILE COMPRESSION)

To save disk space, you can "zip" a file. WinZip for Windows 98 is one product that is commonly used to zip files. However, Microsoft has incorporated a similar product, referred to as **File Compression**, into its **Windows 98 Plus! 98** software add-on. If you already own the **Windows 98 Plus! 98** add-on, you can quickly install this feature into your version of Windows 98. However, if you have not purchased the **Windows 98 Plus! 98** add-on package, then it is strongly recommended that you acquire a copy of WinZip. A fully functioning demo version of WinZip can be downloaded from the Internet at http://www.winzip.com (although you really should license it, which can be done at the reasonable cost of about $35).

INDEX

A

accessing options, 1-2
Active Desktop, 3
   Customize My Desktop command, 4
   customizing, 4-5
   starting, 4
   Wizard, 5
adapters, networks, 135
Add New Hardware Wizard, 6-9
Add Printer Wizard, 10-12
Add Programs (Start menu), 193-194
Add to Favorites command (Favorites menu), 68
Add to Favorites dialog, 68
Add/Remove Programs, 13-16
Add/Remove Programs Properties dialog, 14
adding. *See also* inserting
   clients, 136
   network adapters, 135
   Speed Dial List, 170-171
   tasks (Scheduled Task Manager), 187-188
   toolbars, 202
address books (Outlook Express), 144-147
Address toolbar, 205
addresses, LINKLOCAL network IP, 109
America Online, 17
AOL (America Online), 17
applications
   installing, 13-15. *See also* Add/Remove Programs
   shortcuts, 189-191
   uninstalling, 16
associations (files), 73-75
AT&T WorldNet Service, 18
audio, 192-193. *See also* sounds

B

backgrounds, 43
Backup, 20. *See also* saving
   files, 20-23
BackUp Job Options dialog, 23

BackUp Progress dialog, 22
bitmaps (Paint), 164-165. *See also* graphics
Briefcase, 23
  executing, 24

C

cable, 48
  Direct Cable Connection, 48-49
Calculator, 25
CD Player, 26
centronix cables, 10
  printing, 10-12, 172
changing. *See* modifying
Channel bars, 27, 206
  executing, 27-29
channels, 3, 27. *See also* Active Desktop
  executing, 27-29
  subscribing, 28
Character Maps, 29
characters, 29
chatting, 32
  Comic Chat, 32-35
  NetMeeting, 128-132
clients
  networks, 136
  Outlook Express Email, 148-155
Clipboard, 30
  Viewer, 30

closing
  HypertTerminal, 93
  Windows 98, 31, 191
CODEC (Compression/Decompression), 31
Comic Chat, 32
  configuring, 32-35
  NetMeeting, 128-132
commands
  Active Desktop, Customize My Desktop, 4
  Edit menu, Speed Dial, 170
  Favorites menu, Add to Favorites, 68
  File menu, Export, 200
  Games menu, Deal, 88
  Options menu, Run, 99
  Programs menu
    Games, 87
    HyperTerminal, 91
  Settings menu
    Control Panel, 2, 38
    Printers, 10
  Subscription menu, Subscribe, 28
  Tools menu, Properties, 170
  View menu
    Java Console, 104
    Scientific, 25
    Toolbar, 26

compressing drives, 58
　DriveSpace,
　　executing, 59
Compression Agent, 37
　scheduling, 111-115
Compression Wizard, 58
Compression/
　Decompression, 31
CompuServe, 37
Computer Name, 35-36
configuring. *See also*
　customizing; preferences
　Active Desktop, 4-5
　Comic Chat, 32-35
　Date/Time, 42
　Dial-Up Networking,
　　44-46
　Dial-Up Server, 47-48
　Direct Cable
　　Connection, 48-49
　email, 111
　game controllers, 88-89
　keyboards, 106-107
　modems, 122
　mouse, 124-126
　NetMeeting, 129-132
　networks, 134-135
　　adapters, 135
　　clients, 136
　telephony, 203-204
　time, 204-205
　user profiles, 212
　Workgroup Name, 229

connections
　disconnecting, 93
　HyperTerminal, 92-94
conserving energy, 171-172
Control Panel, 38-41
　command (Settings
　　menu), 38
Control Panel command
　(Settings menu), 2
controllers, games, 88-89
copying files, 71
　Clipboard, 30
　Clipboard Viewer, 30
Create (shortcut), 189-191
Create Shortcut Wizard, 190
credits, 63. *See also* Easter
　Egg
Critical Update
　Notification, 226-227
Customize My Desktop
　command (Active
　Desktop menu), 4
customizing. *See also*
　configuring; preferences
　Active Desktop, 4-5
　channels, 28
　Comic Chat, 32-35
　Date/Time, 42
　Dial-Up Networking,
　　44-46
　Dial-Up Server, 47-48

Direct Cable Connection, 48-49
email, 111
game controllers, 88-89
keyboards, 106-107
modems, 122
mouse, 124-126
NetMeeting, 129-132
networks, 134-135
   adapters, 135
   clients, 136
telephony, 203-204
time, 204-205
user profiles, 212
Workgroup Name, 229

D

databases, Registry, 180-182
Date/Time, 42
Date/Time Properties dialog, 42
deal command (Game menu), 88
Delete (shortcut), 189-191
deleting
   Add/Remove Programs, 13-16
   applications, 16
   deleting, 71-72
   files
      Disk CleanuUp, 50-52
   files/folders, 175-176

   Recycle Bin, 175-176
   fonts, 82
   shortcuts, 191
   Windows 98, 209
desktop, 42. *See also* Active Desktop
   themes, 43
Desktop toolbar, 206
devices, Plug and Play, 7
Dial-Up Networking, 44-46, 103
dial-up networking, 5
Dial-Up Server, configuring, 47-48
dialing
   Phone Dialer, 169-170
   Speed Dial List, 170-171
dialog boxes
   Add to Favorites, 68
   Add/Remove Programs Properties, 14
   BackUp Job Options, 23
   BackUp Progress, 22
   Date/Time Properties, 42
   Display Properties, 5, 54
   Enter Network Password, 217
   Infrared Monitor, 96
   Keyboard Properties, 107
   Modify Channel Usage, 28
   My Connections, 45
   Network, 36, 214

Properties, 2
Regional Settings, 176
TCP/IP Settings, 46
Digital Versatile Disc, 59
Direct Cable Connection
   configuring, 48-49
   wizard, 49
disconnecting
  HyperTerminal
  connections, 93
Disk CleanUp, 50-52
Disk CleanUp, scheduling, 111-115
Disk Defragmenter, 52-54
   scheduling, 111-115
disks
   Compression Agent, 37
   Emergency Startup, 63
     creating, 64-65
display options, 54-56
Display Properties
   dialog, 5, 54
document templates, 57
DOS (Disk Operating System), upgrading from, 100
Drive Converter (FAT32) Wizard, 66
drives
   compressing, 58-59
   Compression Agent, 37
   networks, 138
DriveSpace, 58
   executing, 59

DUN (dial-up networking), 5
DVD (Digital Versatile Disc) Player, 59

E

Easter Egg, 61
   finding, 62-63
Edit menu commands, Speed Dial, 170
Editing Speed Dial List, 170-171
electronic mail. *See* email
email, 61
   configuring, 111
   Outlook Express
     client, 148-155
     maintenance, 156-158
Emergency Startup Disk, 63
   creating, 64-65
Enter Network Password dialog, 217
executing
   Add a Printer Wizard, 10-12
   Briefcase, 24
   CD Player, 26
   Channel bar, 27-29
   Disk Defragmenter, 53-54
   DriveSpace, 58-59
   Network Neighborhood, 137-138

exiting
  HyperTerminal, 93
  Windows 98, 31, 191
Explorer, 221-222
export command
  (File menu), 200
extensions, files, 73-75

F

FAT32, 58
  converter, 66
Favorites, 67-68
  menu commands, Add to Favorites, 68
File menu commands, Export, 200
files
  associations, 73-75
  BackUp, 20
    starting, 20-23
  Clipboard, 30
  Clipboard Viewer, 30
  compressing, 235
  Compression Agent, 37
  deleting, 50-52
  Disk Defragmenter, 52-54
  documents templates, 57
  FAT32, 66
  Internet, 77-78
  managing, 69-72
  Quick View, 174
  Recycle Bin, 175-176
  searching, 75-80
FilterKeys, 1
Find, 75
  files/folders, 75-80
finding. *See also* searching
  Easter Egg, 62-63
  files/folders, 75-81
  Internet files, 77-78
  network computers, 78-79
  people, 79-80
folders
  Favorites, 68
  Recycle Bin, 175-176
  searching, 75-81
fonts, 81-82
Free Cell, 87. *See also* games
freeing hard drive space, 37. *See also* Compression Agent
FrontPage Express, 82-86

G

Game menu commands, Deal, 88
games, 87
  command (Programs menu), 87
  controllers, 88-89
  Free Cell, 87
  Hearts, 87

Minesweeper, 87
Solitaire, 87
starting, 87
GMT (Greenwich Mean Time), 42
graphical user interface, 230
graphics
 bitmaps (Paint), 164-165
 Kodak imaging, 108
 Paint, 164-165
Greenwich Mean Time, 42
GUI (graphical user interface), 230
guides, Online user's, 142

H

hard drives, Compression Agent, 37
hard-disks, FAT32, 66
hardware
 requirements, 90
 system properties, 194-196
 Windows 98 installation, 97-98
Hearts, 87. *See also* games
help, 91
 Kodak imaging, 108
high contrast, 2
HTML (HyperText Markup Language), 3
 FrontPage Express, 82-86

hyperlinks, Favorites, 67-68
HyperTerminal, 91, 103
 connections, 92-94
 disconnecting, 93
 exiting, 93
HyperText markup Language. *See* HTML
HyperTerminal command (Programs menu), 91

I

infrared, 95-96. *See also* wireless
 properties, 95-96
Infrared Monitor dialog, 96
inserting. *See also* adding
 clients, 136
 network adapters, 135
 Speed Dial List, 170-171
 tasks (Scheduled Task Manager), 187-188
 toolbars, 202
installing
 AOL, 17
 applications, 13-16. *See also* Add/Remove Programs
 AT&T WorldNet Service, 18
 CompuServe, 37
 fonts, 81
 infrared components, 95-96

MSN, 117-118
Personal Web Server, 167-168
Prodigy Internet, 173
WaveTop Data Broadcasting, 215-216
Windows 98, 96-98
    DOS, 100
    Windows 3.1, 99
    Windows 95, 98
Integrated Services Digital Network. *See* ISDN
interface, Active Desktop, 3-5
Internet
    files, 77-80
    Profile Manager, 233
    providers, 77, 109
Internet Connection Wizard, 150
Internet Explorer, 100-101
Internet service provider. *See* ISP
IP (Internet Provider), LINKLOCAL network addresses, 109
ISDN (Integrated Services Digital Network), 102
    Connection Wizard, 102
ISP (Internet service provider), 77
    installing, 118
    Prodigy Internet, 173

J

Java, 104-105
Java Console command (View menu), 104
joysticks, 88-89

K

Keyboard Properties dialog, 107
keyboards, 106-107
Kodak imaging, 108

L

LAN (local area network), 5
LapLink, 48
Link toolbar, 206-207
LINKLOCAL network IP addresses, 109
links, shortcuts, 189-191
lists, Speed Dial, 170-171
local area network, 5
logging
    off Windows 98, 110
    onto Windows 98, 110

M

mail, electronic. *See* email
maintenance, Outlook Express Email, 156-158
Maintenance Wizard, 111-115
Make Compatible utility, 115-117

Make New Connection
  Wizard, 44
managing
  files, 69-72
  power, 171-172
  scheduled tasks, 187-188
mapping network
  drives, 138
Media Player, 126, 222
menus, Start, 193
messages. 155. *See also* email
Microsoft Management
  Console, 232-235
Microsoft Network.
  See MSN
Microsoft Paint, 164-165
Microsoft Plus! 98, 119
Microsoft Systems
  Management Server,
  232-233
Minesweeper, 87. *See also*
  games
MMC (Microsoft
  Management Console),
  232-235
modems, 120-122
Modify (shortcut), 189-191
Modify Channel Usage
  dialog, 28
modifying
  display options, 54-56
  file associations, 74
  passwords, 165-166
  sounds, 192-193

monitoring Resource Meter,
  184-185
mouse, 123-126
MouseKeys, 2
moving
  Clipboard, 30
  Clipboard Viewer, 30
  copying files, 71
MSN (Microsoft Network),
  117-118
  installing, 117
  multi-language
    support, 126
multimedia properties, 126
My Computer, 126
My Connections dialog, 45

N

navigating applications,
  189-191
Net Watcher, 127-128
NetMeeting, 128-132
Network dialog, 36, 214
Network interface
  cards, 135
networks, 133-135
  adapters, 135
  clients, 136
  computers, 78-79
  drives, 138
  LINKLOCAL IP
    addresses, 109
  Net Watcher, 127-128
  Network Neighborhood,
    137-138

protocols, 138-139
services, 140
VPN, 213-214
newsgroups, Outlook Express, 158-163
NICs (Network interface cards), 135
NotePad, 141

O

ODBC (Open Database Connectivity), 143-144
online services. *See* ISP
Online User's Guide, 142
Open DataBase Connectivity, 143-144
opening. *See also* starting
  accessibility options, 2-3
  Active Desktop, 4
  BackUp, 20-23
  Calculator, 25
  Clipboard Viewer, 30
  FAT32 converter, 66
  games, 87
  help, 91
  Hyperterminal, 91
    connections, 92-94
  Internet Explorer, 100-101
  Windows 98, 194
operating systems, 175. *See also* Windows 98

options, 1-3
Options menu commands, Run, 99
Outlook Express
  Address Book, 144-147
  Email Client, 148-155
  maintenance tasks, 156-158
  newsgroups, 158-163

P

Paint, 164-165
parallel cables, 49
parallel printer cables, 10
printing, 10-12, 172
passwords, 165-166
PC Card, 166
PCMCIA (Personal Computer Manufacturers Card International Association), 166
Personal Computer Manufacturers Card International Association, 166
Personal Web Server, 167-169
Phone Dialer, 169-170. *See also* dialing
  Speed Dial List, 170-171
pictures. *See also* graphics
  bitmaps (Paint), 164-165
  Kodak imaging, 108
  Paint, 164-165

Plug and Play, 7
Plus 98!, 119
ports, 11
power management, 171-172
preferences. *See also* configuring; customizing
　Active Desktop, 4-5
　Comic Chat, 32-35
　Date/Time, 42
　Dial-Up Networking, 44-46
　Dial-Up Server, 47-48
　Direct Cable Connection, 48-49
　email, 111
　game controllers, 88-89
　keyboards, 106-107
　modems, 122
　mouse, 124-126
　NetMeeting, 129-132
　networks, 134-135
　　adapters, 135
　　clients, 136
　telephony, 203-204
　time, 204-205
　user profiles, 212
　Workgroup Name, 229
printers, 172
Printers command (Settings menu), 10
printing, 10-12, 172
Prodigy Internet, 173
Profile Manager, 233
profiles, user, 210-212
Programs menu commands
　Games, 87
　HyperTerminal, 91
programs. *See* applications
properties
　modems, 120-122
　mouse, 123-126
　multimedia, 126
　sound, 192-193
　system, 194-196
　taskbar, 201-202
　telephony, 203-204
Properties command (Tools menu), 170
Properties dialog, 2
protocols
　networks, 138-139
　TCP/IP, 203

Q

Quick launch, 174
Quick Launch toolbar, 207-208
Quick View, 174

R

readers, 158-163
Recycle Bin, 175-176
Regional Settings, 176
　dialog, 176
registering Windows 98, 177, 179

Registry, 180-182
removing. *See* deleting
renaming shortcuts, 190
requirements
   hardware, 90
   Windows 98 installation, 97-98
Resource Kit, 223
Resource Meter, 184-185
restarting Windows 98, 175
Run, 185
Run command (Options menu), 99
running. *See* executing

S

saving files, 20-23
ScanDisk, 186-187
   scheduling, 111-115
Scheduled Task Manager, 187-188
Scheduling maintenance, 111-115
scientific calculator, 25
Scientific command (View menu), 25
screen savers, 55, 188-189.
   display options, 54-56
searching. 75. *See also* finding
   files/folders, 75-81
   folders, 81
   Internet files, 77-78

network computers, 78-79
   people, 79-80
security
   Net Watcher, 127-128
   passwords, 165-166
selecting screen savers, 188-189
serial cables, 49
servers. *See also* DUN
   Dial-Up, 47-48
   Personal Web, 167-169
services, networks, 140
settings, Regional, 176
Settings menu commands
   Control Panel, 2, 38
   Printers, 10
Setup, Comic Chat, 32
shortcuts, 189-191
   deleting, 191
   renaming, 190
ShowSounds, 1
signing up. *See* installing
SMS (Microsoft Systems Management Server), 232-233
Solitaire, 87. *See also* games
sounds
   properties, 192-193
   Volume Control, 214
SoundsSentry, 1
special characters
   deleting, 82
   installing, 81

Speed Dial
 command
  (Edit menu), 170
 List, 170-171
Start menu, 193
 Add Programs, 193-194
starting. See also opening
 accessibility options, 2-3
 Active Desktop, 4
 BackUp, 20-21, 23
 Calculator, 25
 Clipboard Viewer, 30
 FAT32 converter, 66
 games, 87
 help, 91
 HyperTerminal, 91
  connections, 92-94
 Internet Explorer,
  100-101
 Windows 98, 194
Startup Disk, 98
Startup Disk
 (Emergency), 63
 creating, 64-65
steering wheels, 88-89
StickyKeys, 1
Subscribe command
 (Subscription menu), 28
subscribing to channels, 28
Subscription menu
 commands, Subscribe, 28

Subscription Wizard, 28
symbols, 29
System File Checker,
 196-199
System Information,
 199-200
system properties, 194-196

T

taskbar properties, 201-202
tasks, managing, 187-188
TCP (Transmission Control
 Protocol/Internet
 Protocol), 203
TCP/IP Settings dialog, 46
telephone calls
 Phone Dialer, 169-170
 Speed Dial List, 170-171
telephony, configuring,
 203-204
television, WebTV, 218-220
templates, document, 57
terminate-and-stay-resident
 programs, 97
text, 30. See also files
 NotePad, 141
themes
 desktop, 43
time, 42. See also Date/Time
 configuring, 204-205
ToggleKeys, 1

Toolbar command (View menu), 26
toolbars, 205-208
 adding, 202
 Address, 205
 Channel Bar, 206
 Desktop, 206
 Link, 206-207
 Quick Launch, 174, 207-208
tools, Make Compatible utility, 115-117
Tools menu commands, Properties, 170
Transmission Control Protocol/Internet Protocol, 46
troubleshooting
 Emergency Startup Disk, 63
 creating, 64-65
 Outlook Express, 156-158
 ScanDisk, 186-187
TSR (terminate-and-stay-resident programs), 97
tunneling protocols, 213-214

U

uninstalling
 applications. 14-16. *See also* Add/Remove programs
 Windows 98, 209

Update, 224-225
upgrading
 DOS to Windows 98, 100
 Windows 3.1 to Windows 98, 99
 Windows 95 to Windows 98, 98
 Windows 98, 209
user profiles, 210-212
user's guides, Online, 142
utilities
 Make Compatible, 115-117
 Net Watcher, 127-128
 Profile Manager, 233
 System File Checker, 196-199
 System Information, 199-200

V

View menu commands
 Java Console, 104
 Scientific, 25
 Toolbar, 26
viewing
 files, 174
 Recycle Bin, 175
views, 4
 customizing, 4-5
virtual machine, 104
Virtual Private Networking, 213-214

VM (virtual machine), 104
volume, CD Player, 26
Volume Control, 214
VPN (Virtual Private Networking), 213-214

W

wallpaper, 43
WaveTop Data Broadcasting, 215-216
WBEM (Web-Based Enterprise Management), 232-234
Web pages (FrontPage Express), 82-86
Web Publishing Wizard, 216-218
Web-Based Enterprise Management, 232-234
WebTV, 218-220
Welcome to Windows, 220-221
Windows commands, Run, 185
Windows 3.1, upgrading from, 99
Windows 95, upgrading from, 98
Windows 98
   closing, 191
   installing, 96-100
   logging off, 110
   logging onto, 110
   registering, 177, 179
   restarting, 175
   starting, 194
   uninstalling, 209
   upgrading, 209
   Welcome to Windows, 220-221
Windows 98 Second Edition, 224
Windows Explorer, 221-222
Windows Management Instrumentation, 232-234
Windows Media Player, 126, 222
Windows Publishing Wizard, 85
Windows Update, 224-225
WinPopup, 227
WinZip, file compression, 235
wireless
   communication, 95-96
   WaveTop Data Broadcasting, 215-216
wizards
   Active Desktop, 5
   Add New Hardware, 6-9
   Add Printer, 10-12
   Compression, 58
   Create Shortcut, 190
   Direct Cable Connection, 49
   Dive Converter (FAT32), 66

Internet Connection, 150
ISDN Connection, 102
Maintenance, 111, 113-115
Make New Connection, 44
Personal Web Server, 167-169
Subscription, 28
Web Publishing, 216-218
Windows Publishing, 85

WMI (Windows Management Instrumentation), 232-234
WordPad, 228
Workgroup Name, 229

X-Z

X-Windows, 230
x86, 230

Y2K (year 2000), 231
ZAIW (Zero Administration Initiative), 232

Zero Administration Initiative, 232
zipped files, 235